Ladies and gentlemen, please welcome Britain's top radish sketcher, clock polisher and inconsiderate lover... yes it's

VIC REEVES BIG NIGHT IN

Written by Vic Reeves and Bob Mortimer

FANTAIL BOOKS
Published by the Penguin Group
Penguin Books Ltd, 27 Wrights Lane, London W8 5TZ, England
Penguin Books USA Inc., 375 Hudson Street, New York, New York 10014, USA
Penguin Books Australia Ltd, Ringwood, Victoria, Australia
Penguin Books Canada Ltd, 10 Alcorn Avenue, Toronto, Ontario, Canada M4V 3B2
Penguin Books (NZ) Ltd, 182–190 Wairau Road, Auckland 10, New Zealand

Penguin Books Ltd, Registered Offices: Harmondsworth, Middlesex, England

First published 1991
10 9 8 7 6 5 4 3 2 1

Compiled and edited by James Brown and Andy Darling

Printed in Great Britain by Severn Valley Press, Mid Glamorgan, Wales

ACKNOWLEDGEMENTS
Photographs: p.15, Novelty Island Verdict (Pictor International); pp.34-35 Hey! Hey! Hey! It's Meat! (The Image Bank); p.29 (bottom), Les's Lunch Club (Ace Photo Agency); p.64, Man With the Stick – Ipswich (Tony Stone Worldwide)

Photographs Tim Ridley: p.5,6,7,8,9,12,13,14,22,23,28,29,30-31,38-39,40-41,44,46-47,48,51, 56-57,60-61,62-63,64

Photographs Derek Ridges: p.18,32-33,52-53

Illustration p.21 by Bob Reed
Cartoons p.9,12,15,17,18,22,26-27,36,38,47,48,50,53,56,61,63 by Nigel Parkinson

Record sleeves courtesy of the following: p.44, The Cure – Polydor; p.45, Public Image Ltd – Virgin; p.45, De la Soul – Big Life; p.45, The Fall – Beggars Banquet

Vic Reeves Big Night In is quite simply one of the best things to happen to the western world since the Versailles Peace Conference (1919). Vic Reeves and Bob Mortimer have as canny an understanding of what the people want as did Sir Stafford Cripps in his early budgets (1948). And though Hitler may have annexed the Rhineland (1936), Vic and Bob 'annexed' a permanent place in the affections of a grateful nation.

I urge everyone interested in the development of international politics to buy this book and swap it for another one.

Michael Palin

Rent-a-Foreword

London, Near Ashford, Kent

THE FOLLOWING PERSONS ARE HEAVILY FEATURED HEREIN...

	VIC	BOB	LES
FULL NAME	James Roderick Moir	Robert Renwick Mortimer	Lesley NHN907E Dixon
BIRTHDAY	24 January 1959	23 May 1959	Unknown
BORN	Leeds	Middlesborough	Unknown due to scanty records
SCHOOL	Eastbourne, Darlington	King's Manor, Middlesborough	None (self-taught/ignorant)
HEIGHT	5' 10 $^1/_2$"	5' 7 $^1/_2$"	5' 11" – 7' 11" (seasonal fluctuation)
FAMILY	One sister	Three brothers	His race is distributed unevenly
FAVOURITE FOOD	Bread + fire = toast	Boiled fish	Mangoes
FAVOURITE BEER	Castlemaine XXXX	Sam Smiths	Allergic to liquids
FIRST JOB	Cancer research	Chicken farm	Spray-painting orchids
FAVOURITE FILM	*Saturday Night, Sunday Morning*	*Star Wars*	*Cling*
BEST TV SHOW	Kilroy	This Morning	None (visually naive)
DRIVES	Norton Commando Motor cycle	BMW K75 Motor cycle	Attaches himself to celebrities' vehicles
FAVOURITE COMEDIAN	Tommy Cockles	Tommy Cockles	No comment
TAILOR	Sidney Charles, Deptford High St Lewis Leathers Grensons	Dunn & Co Lagos Emporium, Peckham	Glaxo Industries Barnard Castle
BEST MOMENT	Buying my first motor bike	Seeing Boro in the Zenith Cup Final at Wembley	Being locked in a spirit-level factory
WORST MOMENT	Being trapped in a trunk of old fish at twelve	When I left cheese on top of the wardrobe	Being stranded in a chive farm
FAVOURITE WORD	Oyster	Haystack	No comment (has no concept of language)
MOST LIKE TO MEET	Pol Pot	Beatrice Dalle	Some double-glazing
FAVOURITE CHARACTER	Donald Stott	Davy Stott	
FAVOURITE CIGARETTE	Silk Cut	Embassy	Superkings
MARRIED	No	No	Yes – to his internal wife, Pat
FIRST RECORD	Voodoo Chile (Jimi Hendrix)	Devil's Answer (Atomic Rooster)	Balkan Shipping Signals Volume 3
AMBITION	To build a lighthouse and win the Isle Of Man TT.	To motorbike down the length of the African continent.	To play his Bontempi in front of Prince Charles
MOTTO	You can lead a horse to water, but you can't use a torch underwater.	War, war is stupid and so are those egg containers you get in the sheets.	

YOU WOULD NOT BELIEVE WHAT'S BEEN GOING ON AROUND HERE...

I belched and caused a marriage to be annulled.

I saw Richard Stilgoe with a wheelbarrow full of milk, running. (I think he must have been late.)

Once a year I walk through a special steel hoop, carrying a set of cutlery made from speech.

I saw a little speck of chocolate on this cowboy's jeans. I got close up and it became a beautiful St Christopher's Cross, and then I changed into a radio wave.

I was drinking a cup of tea, and in it was a load of tiny little Miss Marples doing some formation swimming. You would think it'd be too hot for them!

I blew my nose and two bits of liver came out, with maps of the North and South Pole on them.

I was sitting quietly having a picnic on Dustin Hoffman's nose, when Billy Corkhill out of *Brookside* came up and cut it off!

Richard Briers ran wild with a little Dalmatian on a spade. Hannah Gordon has been putting beetroots through pensioners' letter-boxes.

I saw this taxi being driven by laughing haddocks – probably on their way home from the casino.

All these pigeons flew through my car window and started reading me my rights, then they all turned into jelly, and all that was left was a peanut on the dashboard.

I was talking to this really old document when a piper came into the barn and started brainwashing me into selling pellets to deer.

'Chase me, follow me, be with me,' said the fat boy. I couldn't deny him and ended up living inside a tiny padlock with a bit of the boy's spit.

I put too much Savlon on a cut and blocked up the entire high street.

I was in the park really early this morning, ringing a handbell to wake up rabbits.

I licked this little bit of silver and my face took on the shape of a spear, my wrists began to smell of brick, and this gardener came up and booted me on the chest!

Anyway, this shopkeeper rose up on his hindquarters like a praying mantis and ejaculated, 'I simply don't have the resources to stock Pick 'n' Mix.' So I immediately put my trousers back on and left.

Jean Michel Jarre has been round, trying to convince people that the coast of Scotland is wigglier than the coast of New Guinea.

I was playing snooker with Bury St Edmunds, when he dropped the cue and thousands of cartoon ants marched out in line singing, 'Hey ho, hey ho.'

I was sitting on this nice ripe Stilton, eating cherries and thinking about nothing in particular except apple pips and cotton, when Anna Ford ran past with a tattoo of an Elizabethan ruff on her leg.

I pulled all my veins out through my fingers and sorted them into colours.

I was listening to a record by Bread, when a shire-horse jumped out of one of the grooves, causing an earthquake.

BUT LATER ON WE'LL BE MEETING...

A bunch of communists arguing over who has the most gout.

A rabbit in a girdle, wearing an engagement ring.

Victor Mature in a skimpy nightgown, laughing at a kingfisher's diary (they do put a lot of rubbish in them!)

A gentle giant who will stroke a leaf and weep.

Anna Ford having her hair straightened by a Buddy Holly look-alike.

John Fashanu being attacked by a giant whelk in Ronnie Lane's mobile studio.

Roger Daltrey with some of his trout, which he will dry out with a hairdrier, and then poke some red-hot wires into his belly.

A King Constantine of Greece look-alike, who celebrates his island's heritage by sprinkling blackbird beaks on to a porcelain Labrador.

A woman who juggles the clippings from Billy Cotton and Pol Pot in a barrel full of cruesli.

A Portuguese fisherman who pulls all his hair out and grills it with a delicious cheese topping.

A family of trained puffins that drive a vintage tractor over some olives, without crushing them.

A headmaster from Reading who will dismantle an exact replica of the Kon-Tiki raft and rebuild it in a pickled egg.

A trainee locksmith who dresses as a gnome. He will be riding a flock of sheep through the smallest keyhole in Britain.

A bear with a traffic-cone full of receipts for second-hand carpets. Nice!

Wild Bill Hickock nancying about in a cherry orchard with a doily on his head.

But before we go any further, a big round of applause for some top celebrity secrets:-

1. Rod Hull's hideously deformed arm.
2. Penelope Keith's shed full of stolen tracksuits.
3. Gordon Honeycombe's secret gender.
4. Dennis Norden's plastic finger.

LES

A CONVERSATIONAL HISTORY

Although there are many Les facts, there is really very little consistent information on the history of him. Here's some of what is known.

BACKGROUND

Vic: We found Les in a skip in a railway siding in Cheam.

Bob: There were loads of discarded side-partings and he was cowering in a corner infested with lice.

Vic: No, rice. It was being transported to Bombay to get painted. He was emotionally devoid, but we lured him out with...

Bob: Chestnuts... red-hot chestnuts.

Vic: And a bucket of steam that smelled of spices. I immediately recognized in him the ability to guard kennels.

Bob: I cried for a long time when we first met, then he drank my tears like a little puppy.

Vic: No one knows how old he is... he might be Scottish because there was a cross of St Andrew nearby on a couple of occasions. He will likely metamorphose soon into a mulberry bush with many golden rings on it. He can survive without air. He eats discarded rayon, ice, mangoes, fur, residue of portcullis, and cream, lots of cream. He sleeps in his skip, which has been filled with gravel. We know he came out of the land.

Bob: There's some tie-in with Glaxo Industries.

Vic: His mother was a fertilizer, his father was the land. He won't die – he might turn into electricity and be used by pylons in the Third World.

Bob: I've a feeling he might turn into a cobra when we don't see him.

Vic: He has a vague understanding of liquids and levels, hence the spirit-level. Chives are too elaborate for him to get to grips with. Anything that looks like scribbles. And his wife, Pat, lives inside him.

SOCIAL SKILLS

Bob: Les attempts to befriend wolves. He'll have a bath in Radox with lots of handlebars. He's a naughty fella. He goes into shops...

Vic: ... And tells people his teeth are made out of wood.

Bob: Then barks at them.

Vic: Silently.

Bob: He kills eagles, and anyone involved with the brass industry – he goes for the throat.

Vic: I've never seen a better header of the ball. He's had trials at both Plymouth and Southampton.

Bob: And what an expert ski high-jumper – he's linked to Eddie the Eagle.

Vic: Through tapestry.

Bob: In fact, he appears on the Bijoux Tapestry – he's the one with the helmet on at the start.

PRISON RECORD AND OTHER OCCUPATIONS

Vic: He's got a rigid frame, he doesn't have any talent or anything.

Bob: True, he has no concept of performance at all, other than being able to impersonate Bryan Ferry. He met The Living Carpets in his prison cell, after being arrested for something to do with crabs. He was inside for lying through his teeth to the Mayor of Durham.

Vic: As well as creating unwelcome gases at the Mayor's inauguration. He lunges at Royalty. Various frequencies affect him, that's why dogs are lured to him. He's befriended a bit of armour – a gauntlet that covers the forearm – and often goes to Hampton Court to talk to it. He was also the man in the iron mask, and was then hired by Mounties to patrol the Canadian border for a time, until he dissolved.

Bob: He's available for all adjudicating purposes. If you drew a pie chart of his activities, you'd see he's mainly insulating old folks' homes.

Vic: He rides a golden turtle at the underwater city for the government.

Bob: But he hasn't got an arse.

Vic: His passport occupation reads: Ice Warrior. He's got twenty-seven pounds in the bank in sovereigns, and a bar of gold he stole from Captain Blood when he worked for him as a dam. He's also been hired by the Chilean government as a water-displacement unit. Right now he's belting through a forest in Bombay impressing lasses.

Bob: I like to think he's back in his skip throwing a button at a dead cat.

Vic: After each show all we see is Les and his wolf wandering off into the sunset.

Bob: With writing on his back.

LES FACT ····► Les has a coarse, rasping laugh (but he only laughs at lemons).

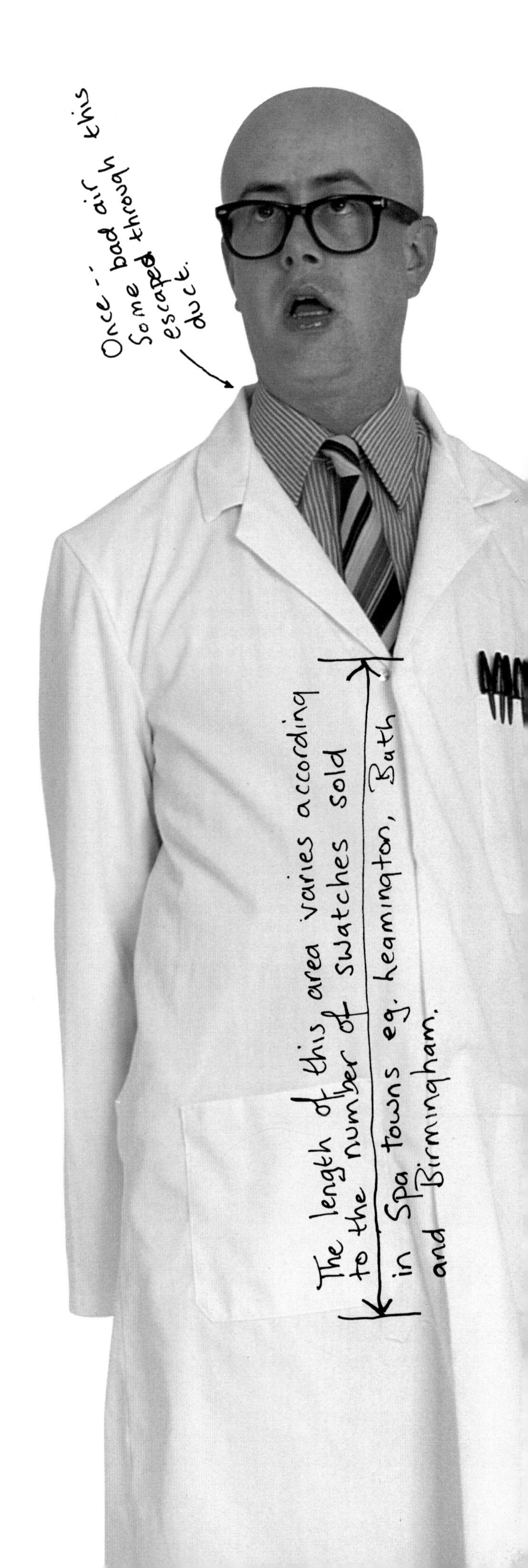

MAN WITH THE STICK INVESTIGATES

Vic: And now, ladies and gentlemen, untie your underpants, stand at the edge of your parish boundary and bind your feet in the Chinese way! Retreat behind enemy lines, inject your Labrador with pigeon fat and then scribble all over the Bible! He's canny, he's cute, his favourite movie's *Klute*! He's friendly, yet ill, he watches *The Bill*! Ladies and gentlemen:
THE MAN WITH THE STICK!

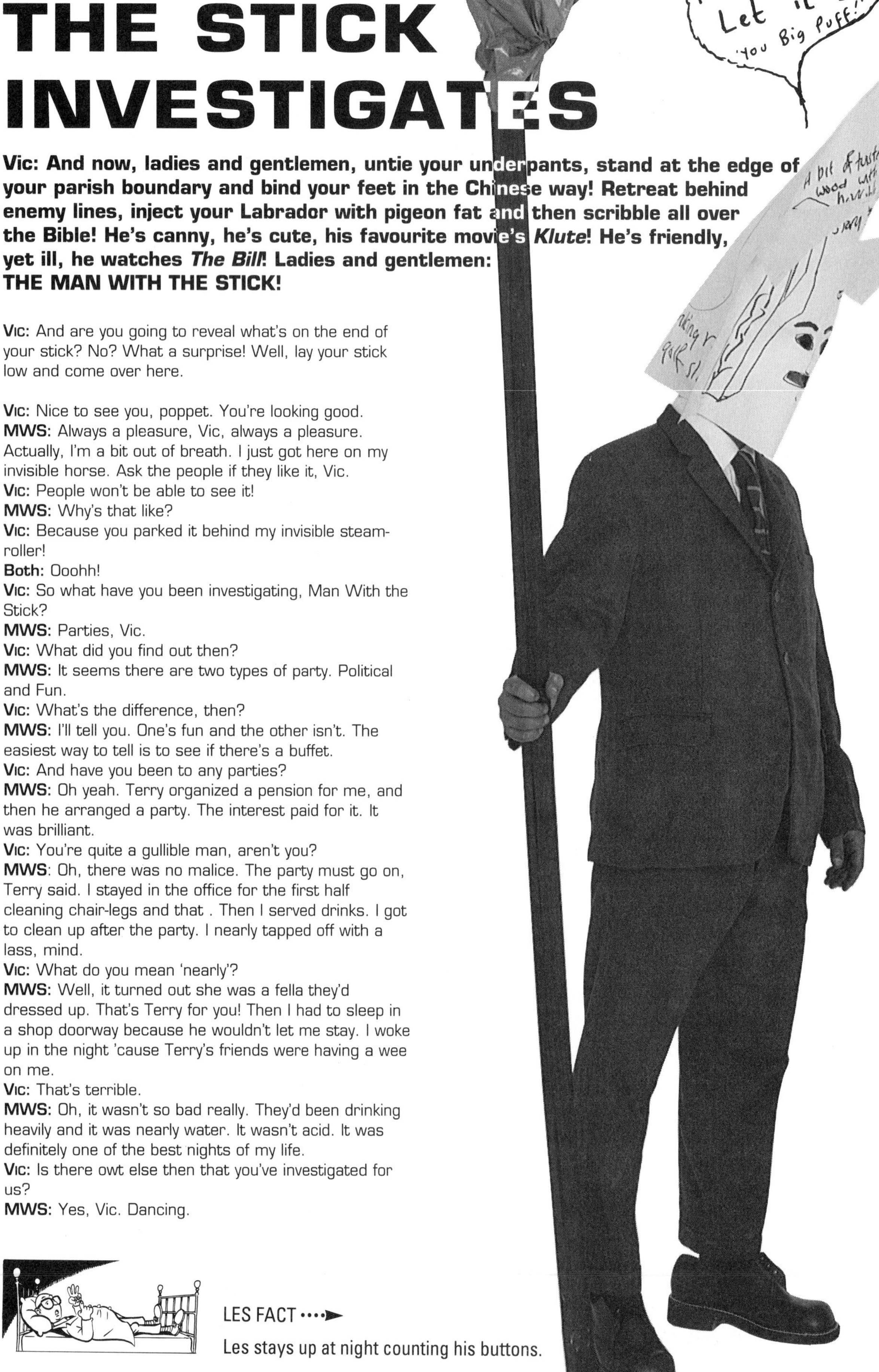

Vic: And are you going to reveal what's on the end of your stick? No? What a surprise! Well, lay your stick low and come over here.

Vic: Nice to see you, poppet. You're looking good.
MWS: Always a pleasure, Vic, always a pleasure. Actually, I'm a bit out of breath. I just got here on my invisible horse. Ask the people if they like it, Vic.
Vic: People won't be able to see it!
MWS: Why's that like?
Vic: Because you parked it behind my invisible steam-roller!
Both: Ooohh!
Vic: So what have you been investigating, Man With the Stick?
MWS: Parties, Vic.
Vic: What did you find out then?
MWS: It seems there are two types of party. Political and Fun.
Vic: What's the difference, then?
MWS: I'll tell you. One's fun and the other isn't. The easiest way to tell is to see if there's a buffet.
Vic: And have you been to any parties?
MWS: Oh yeah. Terry organized a pension for me, and then he arranged a party. The interest paid for it. It was brilliant.
Vic: You're quite a gullible man, aren't you?
MWS: Oh, there was no malice. The party must go on, Terry said. I stayed in the office for the first half cleaning chair-legs and that . Then I served drinks. I got to clean up after the party. I nearly tapped off with a lass, mind.
Vic: What do you mean 'nearly'?
MWS: Well, it turned out she was a fella they'd dressed up. That's Terry for you! Then I had to sleep in a shop doorway because he wouldn't let me stay. I woke up in the night 'cause Terry's friends were having a wee on me.
Vic: That's terrible.
MWS: Oh, it wasn't so bad really. They'd been drinking heavily and it was nearly water. It wasn't acid. It was definitely one of the best nights of my life.
Vic: Is there owt else then that you've investigated for us?
MWS: Yes, Vic. Dancing.

LES FACT ····►

Les stays up at night counting his buttons.

Vic: Dancing, you say?
MWS: That's right. And again there are two main types. There's contemporary, which for a simple fella like you, is modern, and disco.
Vic: Oh, I love disco. Boogaloo, jig-a-jig, skipping and that.
MWS: Do you wear a tight pant yourself then, Vic? And a felt hat?
Vic: I do.
MWS: You'll know all about disco dancing then.
Vic: So what's the difference between contemporary and disco?
MWS: There's a very clear difference. One you get paid for and it's crap, and the other you pay for and it's good.
Vic: So when was dancing invented then?
MWS: Vic, I believe it was in 1973 in a betting shop in Slough. I think the man had won a horse.
Vic: What, and he started jigging about.
MWS: That's right.
Vic: And are there any other types of dancing?
MWS: Yes, there are two other types. There's tea dancing, which you do when you've had a lovely tea, and there's dirty dancing, which you do after hours when you're excited.
Vic: Have you done that, then?
MWS: I haven't, Vic, but I've seen it.
Vic: Have you ever seen *Come Dancing*?
MWS: No, but I've seen some seamen jig!
Vic: Anyway, I think we know all about dancing now. What else have you been looking at?
MWS: Holidays, Vic. Again they seem to fall into two particular types. There's your package deal type. That's a particular phrase used in the industry, meaning you take packages and it's in Deal.
Vic: Got you. What's the other one?
MWS: The other type is the Go-As-You-Please-Island-Hopping-I'm-Me-Own-Man type. Now for that one you need an itinerary and you need injections.
Vic: So you go to your doctor, do you?
MWS: No, I go to some squatters in the Old Kent Road and get them to inject me.
Vic: What do they inject you with?
MWS: Vic, I don't ask.
Vic: It could be puppy fat.
MWS: I don't ask. I could be puppy fat, yes. When you go abroad, you should always remember to take something to swap with the locals. Anything to do with *Poltergeist 2,* say, or a ball of Robin wool. Or you could take food.
Vic: That sounds interesting. What like?
MWS: Brisket.
Vic: Brisket.
MWS: Mutton.
Vic: Mutton.
MWS: Beef! Anyway Vic, I was wondering, are you still diverting those funds from heart research into your otter fur bookmark project?
Vic: You had to mention it, didn't you? You had to mention my endangered species stationery outlet. You wouldn't let it lie! Take your stick and clear off!
MWS: It's just, I'm reading something at the moment and if there's a bookmark going spare...

THE PLAYS PAGE

Reeves and Mortimer Productions
Top Plays for Peasants

An Historical Play

LANCELOT: Aaaaaahhh! My Lord Cromwell, where are thy henchmen, oh?
CROMWELL: Aaaaaahhh! Lancelot, they be at the match, yes, the match!
LANCELOT: Aaaaaah! Aha! Ho ho!! Well, well, well, my liege.
CROMWELL: Yes, yes.
LANCELOT: Aaaaaaaaaaaaaaaarrrrgghh! Oh, Lord!
CROMWELL: Aaaaaaah, oh ho! My Lord Lancelot, what be thine own men be deeing?
LANCELOT: Oooooh! A! A! A! Jig-a-jig! Hi! Hi! Aaah!
CROMWELL: Mony mony scaramossh, Captain Drake must surrender for thine is the kingdom, nickety nackety, twiddle the knob! Oooh! Hoo! The Mamba!
LANCELOT: Whooaaaaa little rabbit, withy do thee wander, pretty maiden?
CROMWELL: Aye, my Lord, her hair is a pretty colour. Cock-a-doodle-doo aaaaaaaah!
LANCELOT: Aaaaaaaaaaaaaaaaaahhhh!!!
CROMWELL: Aaaaaaaaaaahh!!!
LANCELOT: BINGO!!!

A Play About the Beatles

PAUL: Oh, Ringo!
RINGO: Oh, Paul! How popular we Beatles are.
PAUL: Oh, aye! Ha ha! Yes yes! Oh, Ringo!
RINGO: My drums go 'nik nik nackety nock'!
PAUL: Oh yes, yes aaaaarrghhhh!!!
RINGO: Oh, Paul! The seagull flies like this (demonstrate the flight of the gull).
PAUL: Aaaaaarrrgghhh! Uh! Uh! Uh! Oh!
RINGO: Yes, yes.
PAUL: Oh, Ringo, withy wandereth the pretty maiden thee hath a-courted recent?
RINGO: Aaaaaah! She hath nicked off, son.
PAUL: Oh, oh, oh, oh, oh, ug! ug! ug!
RINGO: Oh, mama, by jingo, pitter patter!
PAUL: Oh, my Lord Wolsey, Agincourt has fallen and I fear the death of Van Gogh.
RINGO: Have courage, Captain Bligh, for soon we join the Swiss Family Robinson.
PAUL: Aaaaaaaaaaaaarrrrrrggghhhh!!!!
BOTH: VICTORY!

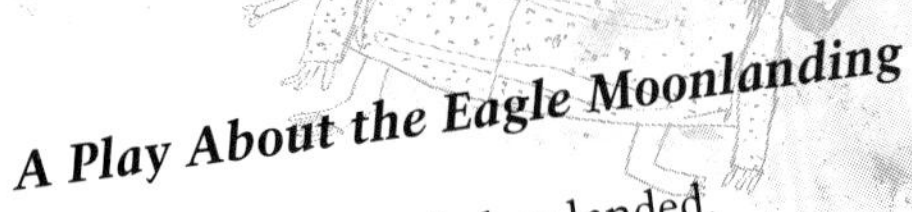

A Play About the Eagle Moonlanding

ARMSTRONG: Oh, Aldrin, the Eagle has landed.
ALDRIN: Aye aye, Cap'n, right away, oh!
ARMSTRONG: Aaaaaaah! Prithy.
ALDRIN: Ooooooooo, get the golf balls, sir!
ARMSTRONG: Aye, there be plenty more where that came from, Tom Dooley.
ALDRIN: Aaaaaarrghh, my Lord, your hair is so soft, baaaaah! Damn you, Mayor of Casterbridge!
ARMSTRONG: Rrraaaaahhh!! By the wings of Allah! Ten thousand curses on this darned module.
ALDRIN: Oh, Johnny, why do you have to fight the Jets tonight?
ARMSTRONG: Aaaaaahrghhhh!!! Balls!
ALDRIN: Ah! Mr Pineapple, I was wondering if you could have the books done by five o'clock?
ARMSTRONG: Aaaaaaaaaaaaaarrrrrrgghh!!!!
BOTH: BINGO!

CASSETTE IDENTIFICATION GLOVE*

Simply arrange your cassettes into this configuration, then when you lay the incredible identification gauntlet upon your collection, you can simply read off the titles off the incredible glove.

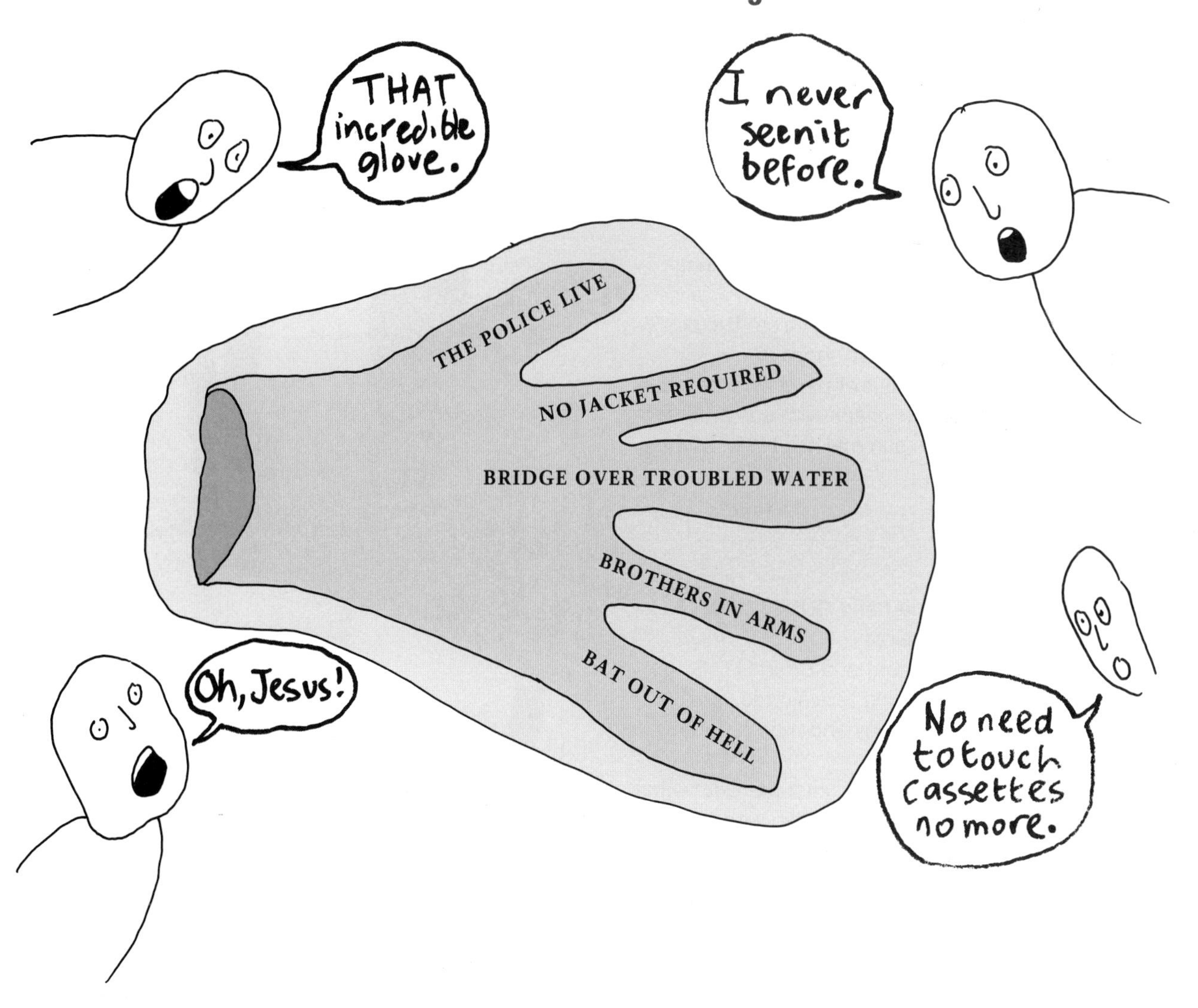

*** CAN ALSO BE CONVERTED INTO DEED POLL GLOVE FOR THE FOLLOWING FIVE NAMES:-**

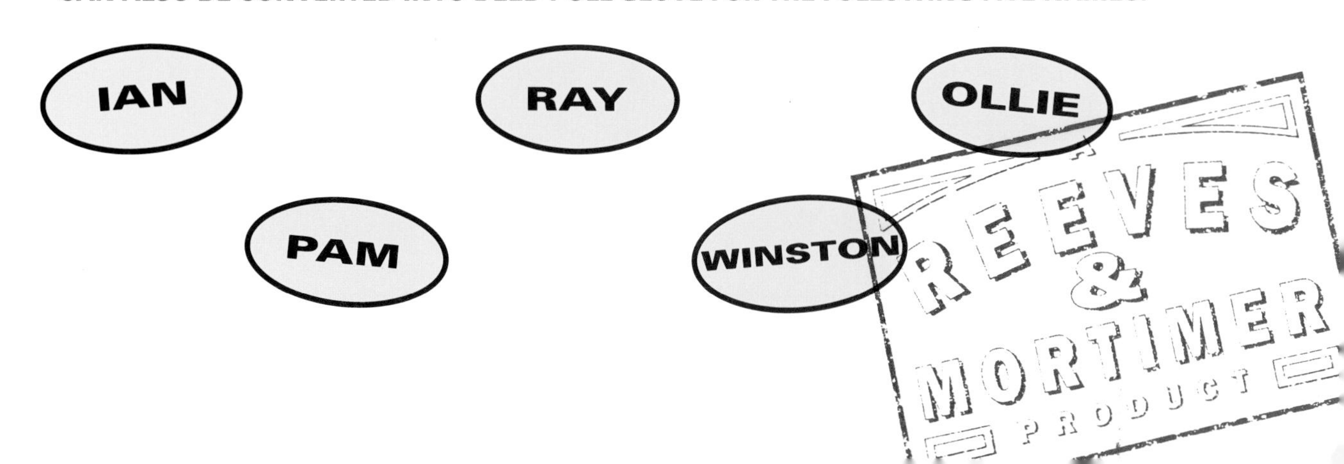

NOVELTY ISLAND CHALLENGE – THE FINALISTS

Act 1
RAY DIXON with SIMON THE SEASONAL SEABIRD
Ray D.O.B. 4/4/44 (Gibson). His favourite memory is when a nice rabbit (not fierce like Schwarzenegger) reared up behind the counter of a tea-shop, and winked at him. His catchphrase is 'Watch it, missis, it's sticky!'

Simon, Ray's pet seabird, will demonstrate the four seasons in the following ways:

a) Spring – spring 'onions' will leap from his lungs when Ray claps once.
b) Autumn – wet leaves will emerge from the bird's backside on hearing Ray clap thrice.
c) Winter – now it's snow out of Simon's eyes when Ray combines seventeen claps with ear drift.
d) Summer – there is no summer for birds, according to Ray.

Act 2
PAT FLATTERTY (Fishwife) and BRIAN GRANT (Ninja Warrior) – Stompers
Pat D.O.B. 4/4/44 (Galosh) and Brian D.O.B. 4/4/44 (Brogue), present a stomping tête-à-tête.

Pat enjoys Sellotaping candy and marshmallows on to trawlers to bring good luck.

Brian is a local Ninja Warrior from the Cotswolds. He enjoys spending time in the kitchen with his wife, Marion, making delicious rum truffles, tarts and franzipans in their seventeenth-century converted chapel.

Here, they stomp to the following records:

PAT
Heated Hairgrips
by Iron Monger
Viper Attack
by Virus
Lung Disorder
by Serum
Ditch
by Air Rifle

BRIAN
Pretty Rainbow
by Sally
Lovely Summer Dress
by Silk and Satin
Oh, Yes, Babbling Brook
by The Coffee and Cream
Lovely Kind Mice
by Image

LES FACT 

Les is inextricably drawn to the mouth-watering taste and texture of Orkney mangoes.

Act 3
WAVY DAVY presents
WHEN YOUR BEST PAL DIES

SEE YA!

Wavy D.O.B. 4/4/44 (Oxford). His earliest memory is waving goodbye to his parents when they abandoned him at Woodall Services on hearing of a cheese sale in Wrexham. His catchprases are as follows:

1) 'See yah'
2) 'Bye'
3) 'Bring us something nice back'
4) 'Don't forget to remember'

Here, Davy hauls a brace of grapes over rough ground representing Patch and Work, his two pet Cairngorm 'Nut' terriers, whom he waved goodbye to when they died giving birth to a blind pheasant in a car coat.

Act 4
GRAHAM LISTER

Graham D.O.B. 4/444/4444 (Chelsea Boot)
Once again, the juvenile rantings of a bitter and twisted talentless hawker of pedantry...
Graham Lister, ACA, BMA, MD, FRCOS. Mr Lister now presents a

Mr Lister now presents a quality piece in stark contrast to the rantings of Workshy Fop Reeves. Mr Lister's proudest memory was his transformation of Cher from a 'gypsy, tramp and thief' into a beautiful actress/vocalist, using his skilled and innovative plastic surgery skills: gorgeous. The technically brilliant piece he presents is called:

SEA, SHELLS AND SURGERY

Lister: Here I give a glimpse into the skilled world of the paediatrician as I use my as yet uncertified surgery techniques.

a) I will perform skilled surgery on four youths.
b) I will take only three skill-filled minutes.
c) I will use only winkle shells, crabsticks and starfish.

Act 5
JUDITH GRANT

Judith D.O.B. 4/4/44 (Slingback)
Her most recent memory is pulling her pants down, farting into a goblet and clubbing a plumber with it! Her catchphrase is 'Who's hiding in there? What do you want? Oh, it's you, Donald. I thought it might be.'

Tonight, Judith hoists her skirt up, farts into a goblet and clubs a cobbler with it.

Act 6
MR WOBBLY HAND

Mr Wobbly Hand D.O.B. 444/44444/44444444 (Canadian log-roller inc. high-'topped, non-slip bully flange with dolly handles.)

No clear memories to report.

He owns a string of strawberry juice/light-bulb shops in Barrow-in-Furnace, including Berries 'n' Bulbs, Thirst at First Light and Spotlight on Strawberries. Since his first appearance on television, he has gone on to re-create the infamous meeting of Friar Tuck and Robin Hood inside a crow's beak.

Welcome back, Mr Wobbly Hand!

Reasons why we have selected six turns:

All good things come in sixes, eg, eggs, tracks on side one of any good LP, tinned hot dogs, the legs on an insect, the lanes on any decent motorway ie the M20, tinned beer, Henry the 8th's wives, bullets in a pistol ie the one used by Doug McClure in *The Virginian*, the beeps on the Greenwich time signal, hexagons, a set of beakers or tumblers, working days of the week, strings on a guitar, the number of hairs on Elton John's head, the dreams of Doctor Sardonicus, ideal number of monkeys in any cage or box, ideal distance in metres between two posts, crack Spanish dance troops, diving gear, the Three Degrees' shoes, old men in parks, beats on a drum prior to an execution, treasure maps, police in attendance at serious fire eg department store, photographs of daggers, dug outs trenches and pits, and, of course, the ideal number of hours of preparation before drilling a hole.

ACTS THAT DIDN'T MAKE IT TO NOVELTY ISLAND:

Among the acts knocked out in the earlier nationwide preliminary rounds were the following: Ronnie Barrett and His Floury Fingers • Kenneth Tanner the Illegal Taper • The Dampener • Billy Buildings (The Building Impersonator) • Mr Adhesion • Eggo • The Price Slasher • Man With a Bubbly Temperament and a Tiny Claw • The Fudge Packer • Man Who Unrolls a Swiss roll, puts it on his face and gouges out two eyeholes and a mouth hole. He then performs 'The Farmyard at Dawn' and 'Carbon Monoxide, wot Carbon Monoxide?' • The Man Who Puts Marmalade on to Birds' Beaks • Rev Collins – he can get 200 mph out of a sheepdog • Paul McCartney and Linda • Gay Toreador • Half Man, Half Squirrel – he buries nuts • Man With a Lost Tribe of Pygmies near his nipple – they're not Pygmies, they're ants. • Tony Toaster – he has a brown back and a buttered apron • I Am a Prisoner sings 'Not guilty' • Crutchy The Mole (he has a crutch) • Last night a DJ grilled my hair – Mr J Frost • Birthday gifts made from dog dirt – Eileen Sadler • Ian Baird The Yeoman, with Rusty The Whistling Raven • Pat Flatterty and His Dancing Poodles (Not quite good enough) • Mr Melons • Man who feels uneasy in the presence of Paul McCartney, but unbelievably doesn't recognize Phil Collins • Mr 45 with Romantic Raymonde (great angles, etc) • Arctic Explorers • Carl Pearce, the Glove Collector • Pear Burner ('Oh, what a lovely pear', Loopy Tom from Aldershot.) • Humming Igloos, presented by Gloria Drummond • Kung Fu Rabbit operated by a drunk (Jean Luc-de-Gard) • Pancake and Bottom Pincher – give recipe to unit trust manager and have bottom pinched • Tom Murray (not mint) • Johnny Vitriol.

Late Entries
(Disqualified).

Den Powell and his 'conjugal' Abacus.

Curtis Lamb and his unique 'pelmet Destruction' Abacus.

Lynn Barber with her mirrored abacus (It removes make-up).

Russell the Pigeon and his advice pack for small Businesses.

'I'm only a little Boy, Sir' by Mr George Long.

Doug Parsons and his formica foot clamp.

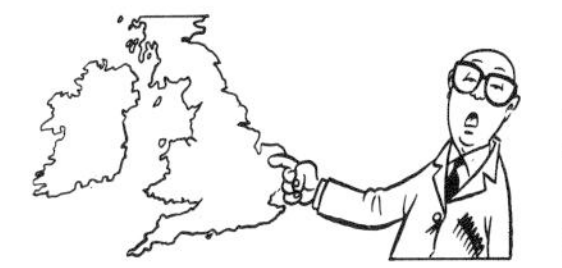

LES FACT

Les thinks Cardiff is in East Anglia.

THE VERDICT

Mayor of Casterbridge: Hello, Mayor of Casterbridge here, speaking from a telephone box perched precariously on top of the North Cliff at Whitby. I have a marvellous panoramic view of the northern coastline almost as far as Saltburn. Joining me in the telephone box are Cameo and The Stylistics. We're here doing our bit for the 'Clean Up Britain's Coastline' Campaign, along with The Chi-Lites, The Temptations, The Tams, The Isley Brothers (right bunch o' jokers, those guys!), The Four Tops, The Miracles (Smokey's working on the west coast), The Pips, Hot Chocolate…er…

Vic: Wait on, Mayor. So now you've been watching Novelty Island, which has been piped through to you via a network of mirrors and lenses perched strategically along Britain's coastline. Which top turn have you selected to block up 'Old Peculiar', the enormous effluent overflow at Filey?

Mayor of Casterbridge: Well, we'll be using Graham Lister. His woolly hairdo should mop it up effortlessly.

Vic: So, Graham it is. Now, whilst I've got you, Mayor, is it true that the real reason behind your Clean Up Britain's Coastline Campaign is it's a promotional gimmick for your new Motown compilation?

Bzzzzzzzzzzzzzzzzzzzzzzzzz

'INDY'

SONG PAGES

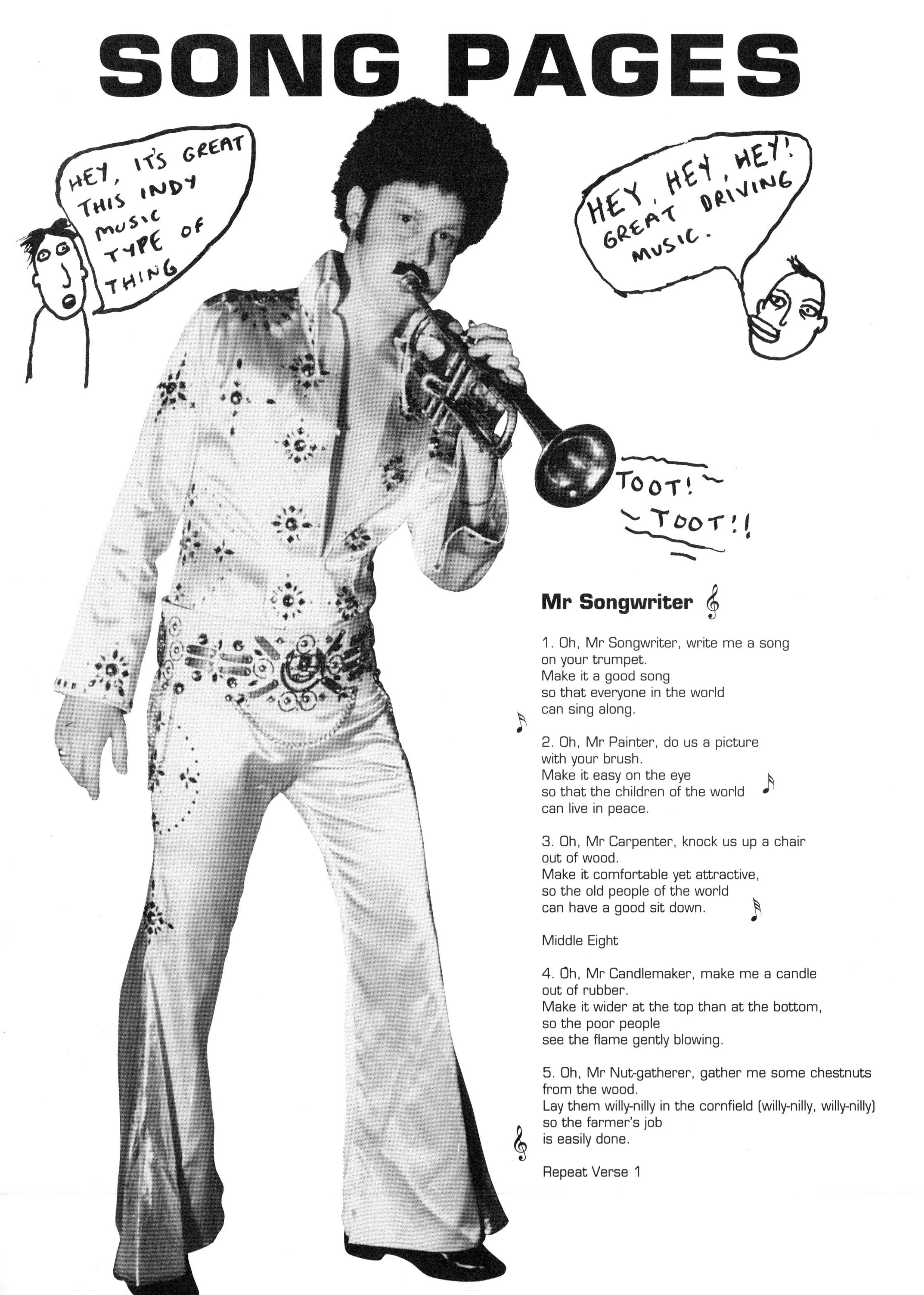

Mr Songwriter

1. Oh, Mr Songwriter, write me a song
on your trumpet.
Make it a good song
so that everyone in the world
can sing along.

2. Oh, Mr Painter, do us a picture
with your brush.
Make it easy on the eye
so that the children of the world
can live in peace.

3. Oh, Mr Carpenter, knock us up a chair
out of wood.
Make it comfortable yet attractive,
so the old people of the world
can have a good sit down.

Middle Eight

4. Oh, Mr Candlemaker, make me a candle
out of rubber.
Make it wider at the top than at the bottom,
so the poor people
see the flame gently blowing.

5. Oh, Mr Nut-gatherer, gather me some chestnuts
from the wood.
Lay them willy-nilly in the cornfield (willy-nilly, willy-nilly)
so the farmer's job
is easily done.

Repeat Verse 1

LES FACT ····►

Les once chased Sarah Brightman into a cheese shop!

Warhol

You lived your life like a knife,
cutting through red tape and painting it white
at night, it's all right . . . you were right.
You painted soup tins when it wasn't in
to paint soup tins.
Your wig was bright white
like you'd had a fright
off a ghost or summat.
You died a violent death, like your life –
why did the brakes fail on that hot night in
Monte Carlo?
Could it have been the adverse weather conditions
or was it interference from a jealous painter in
your peer group?
What were your last thoughts –
can they be bought?
Or are they 'Not For Sale' like your pictures?

Chorus
Why, oh why, did you go away
On that sunny winter's day?
What made you take the flight
that took your life that hot summer night?

I Remember Punk Rock

Chorus
I remember punk rock
like it was only yesterday,
Oh, Mr Buzzcock on my shoulder
singing in that extra-special way.
Oh yes, I remember punk rock,
I recall all those melodies
by The Clash, The Adverts, Wire, Eater,
not to mention ATV.

1. Generation X sang so sweetly
whilst The Pistols ate their lunch.
The Damned had tea with The Lurkers,
As X-Ray Spex enjoyed brunch.

Chorus and Whistle

2. The Vibrators sang so tenderly
while 999 had soup.
Richard Hell had The Slits round for coffee
and Slaughter and The Dogs round too.

Chorus and Whistle

An Empty Kennel

He was a friend and a hairy companion
two big brown eyes staring at the sun.
His tail would wag in the summer breeze
and gently caress my cheeks.

The swimming-pool attendants couldn't save him –
That old fella just weighed too much.
He waved goodbye as he sank out of sight
like a crab in a workman's lavy.

But now that old kennel is empty,
though I might use it for storing engine parts.
If I blocked up the hole and turned it upside down
I could use it as a coracle.
But for now I'll just use it for private reasons,
at midnight when the moon is full
and I hope to use it tonight with you
And you and you and you
In fact, all of yous.

The New Romantic

1. Oh, for the New Romantic
sitting alone at his weaving-loom,
slowly weaving lace collars
to the sound of a big bass drum.

2. Sing hi! For the New Romantic
and the peacock feather in his cap,
silver buckles rattling,
frilly shirts flapping in the breeze.

3. Spare a thought for the New Romantic
as he crimps his fringe till dawn
using a sandwichmaker
to the sound of a flugelhorn.
Fade to grey.

1. Remember the clouds are your friends too.
They're just there to stop the sky gettin' blue.
So if your feelin' down just lie on your back
And look up at the sun for a laughter attack.

Chorus:
Everybody's laughing at the sun
Everybody's creased up at his age
He's just a great big hot ball of Fun
Parsley, Thyme, Rosemary and Thyme.
x 80

IT'S NOT ALL WALKING

'Hello, I'm Alan Wright.'
'And I'm Alan Parsons, and this is my project for the week.'
'We're going on a sponsored walk and who's our sponsor, Alan?'
'Well, Alan, it's the Air-Tight Tea-Bag Company.'
'And you've had a new business idea, haven't you, Alan?'
'I'm going to package oxygen cheaper than them. I'm going to go down to Brighton with a cup and get some nice sea air, put a bit of Clingfilm over it and sell it.'
'You'll need an order first, won't you?'
'Who needs air? I'll go to America in a van, reverse it up and get some warm air in the back, then return to the butchers and defrost their beef. And do it a lot cheaper than BOC.'
'So we're going on our sponsored walk to Arscarfengarfensdale.'
'You know, we're a very familiar sight up on Arscarfengarfensdale, with the rabbits and so forth.'
'The little fishes pop their eyes out when we pass. There's quite a good strong mist up there sometimes, which means you can be enshrouded in mist and get away with quite a lot. I remember one time we went up with my wife, Mary. And we were so enshrouded in mist, you both came back with each other's clothes on. Why was that?'
'We had made a shelter, like you taught us, Alan. And her clothes got very damp . . . and I offered to wear them because I know how much I care for . . . you care for her. Oooh, she thrashed about in that bracken. I tried to control her, there was a terrible smell.'
'Probably one of those little tomatoes you grow. I caught Alan in the greenhouse once showing my wife, Mary, his tomato plants and a lovely little ripe red one he had in his hand, as well.'
'You looked over my shoulder and saw us admiring my lovely ripe red cherry tomato. Another time Alan found some Roman coins in his garden . . .'
'And you took them away to be valued and they were . . .'

LES FACT

Les once followed a gypsy for 5 miles!

'Absolutely worthless.'
'That'll be about the time you won the pools.'
'And I took Mary with me to Portugal.'
'You went on an archaeological dig with her, didn't you?'
'Hmmm, we had to share a cabin. Do you remember that story, about the ticket mix-up? So it's not all walking.'
'We saw The Style Council on our sponsored walk, inspecting a style.'
'And Joe Cocker . . . and we had one of your games of I Spy, Alan.'
'Yes, Alan, I spied something beginning with AA.'
'And I thought it was that AA van we saw parked by the road.'
'But it wasn't, it was that AA Milne crouching in a bush.'
'And what were you doing with Mary whilst I was studying that tree-oyster?'
'Well, Alan, a little mouse wearing a 007 wristwatch popped out of the ground near Mary. She was startled, and fell, hurting her thigh.'
'But, Alan, you were all over her!'
'She'd also been bitten by a swan. It was after that perfume I gave her.'
'That Quail Spore Cologne?'
'I don't know why you were so furious, Alan.'
'I wasn't furious – I was alerting you.'
'To our time-and-distance experiments.'
'Because it's not all walking, Alan.'
'It's not all bloody walking, it never has been, it never will.'

The Country Code

NEVER shout at widows or needles.

NEVER frighten turtles with dubbin.

REMEMBER the badger has his problems too, and don't you doubt it. He just needs a shoulder to cry on, and, crikey, why shouldn't he be our brother too?

REMEMBER the heron is your brother too, and just needs a shoulder to cry on and a kind word.

REMEMBER, clever as he is, the wise old owl needs friends and a little love and understanding.

GIVE a little space to sister pigeon and cousin sycamore; they just need a little peace and quiet.

IF you start a fire, put a pasty on it quick.

WHEN dropping litter, always sweep it under a bush.

NEVER deliberately offend the farmer's wife.

WHEN in a cornfield, always check your passage is clear.

ALWAYS wear gloves when handling cattle.

REMEMBER courting couples have right of way.

NEVER carry on in a barn or at harvest-time.

FLIP-flops, lip gloss, pom-poms, tutu, boob tubes, pop sox, jim-jams, knapsacks, handbags and, of course, cufflinks.

~A Child's Story~

t was a warm summer's evening and little Timmy Tittlemonger, the scampering water-rat, was digging a hole to bury a dead wasp he'd recently killed with an old cup handle. When all of a sudden, little Johnny Humbug The Bumblebee buzzed along in his army jeep made of acorns and sesame seeds and powered by buttercup gas.

'Oh ZZ, Timmy ZZ,' cried Johnny Humbug. 'You must ZZ help me ZZZ, my uncle Tommy Truffles, who as you know is a ZZZ bluebird, has got his wing lodged under the pendulously skinned area 'twixt udder and inner thigh ZZZ of Old Mrs Plumpton the cow of Willoughby Chase.'

'Oh, calamity!' ejaculated Timmy. 'I'll bring my oxy-acetylene welding equipment made from blueberries and water-lillies, and my helmet made from strawberry pips and puff pastry, that should do the trick!'

So off they scampered to the scene of the wing-lodgement incident. No sooner had they arrived, when they saw old Farmer Partridge approaching the wing-lodgement area with Randy Old Albert, the breeding bull, ready for his Sunday mounting.

'Oh crikey!' buzzed Johnny Humbug, the buzzy old bumblebee. 'We must hurry in order to effect a clean dislodgement before Old Albert begins to service stroke sire.'

They quickly jumped on to the back of Young Lenny the Trout's elderberry-powered helicopter, first checking to see if he had his pilot's licence made from celery leaves and Edam cheese rind, and off they shot, straight to the epicentre of the wing-lodgement brouhaha.

'Oh, oh!' suggested Uncle Tommy Truffles, the wing-lodged bluebird, and they swiftly erected a canopy over the area made famous by the wedged wing, in order for them to work in the artificial light of a cabbage leaf, as it was pleasant to do so.

After initial scaffolding was completed, they swiftly began to bore test-holes in Old Mrs Plumpton's udder, to release pertinent gases and salient juices. By this time, Old Albert had begun the Bonding Ceremony and started to raise his hoofs in order to achieve an effective grip on old Mrs P.

There was no time for extra test-drilling, and Little Timmy Tittlemonger the water-rat unhesitatingly rammed a sharpened celery stalk into the cow's lactic bag.

'Sploosh!' Out came a torrential gush of gorgeous white spume, tossing them to the ground like so many petals from a blossoming cherry tree.

'Oh lovely!' insisted Uncle Tommy Truffles, the previously wing-lodged bluebird. 'How can I thank you enough?'

And they all filled their acorn cups with the milk from the cow.

'What queer-tasting milk this is!' challenged Timmy Tittlemonger, and by the spent look on Old Albert's face, I think he was probably right, wasn't he, children?

A DAY IN THE LIFE OF LISTER

I live a simple life, I don't bother anyone, if they bother me I sue them. The highpoint is receiving forms first thing in the morning. I like order in my life. I don't always get it, especially at the hands of the NHS. I like it when anyone writes to me. Apart from my good friend Mr Dennis the Confectioner Stroke Newsagent, I have no close associates, but people do know me. Dr Christiaan Barnard is a hero of mine, he did the first heart-displacement operation. Dr Hilary Jones, the TV Doctor, is another; I watch him every morning on TV AM. Carol Bordeman the dancer, very beautiful.

Bob Dennis is a lovely man, he manages Aswad you know. I don't like it in restaurants very often. I get up early in the morning because I don't sleep well due to my back and I've often got a lot of forms arriving of a morning. I have a cup of water and a handful of Iced Gems. For the rest of the day I have sweets: Midget Gems, Teddy Bears, Golf Balls, huge Jelly Dolphins, all them. I go to Pick 'n' Mix in Mr Dennis's shop, he doesn't give a discount though. He sells a good sweet. Shrimps, mainly jelly-based sweets. Black Jacks.

Having had my water and Iced Gems, I arrange my mail into shapes, then I watch TV AM. Fools! I go down to the Centre quite often, but I've never got in yet. I want to deliver one of my lectures on stance and posture.

I often open my curtains, well, they're not curtains they're blankets I have hanging up to help prevent damp. I have dampness, I've complained to the local authority about it.

There's my typewriter and I've got that cream-and-blue cutlery. I've got a pan and there's a piece of string where I used to hang it up. There's a lot of strings hanging from the ceiling with pegs on the end for drying documents on. The people upstairs inject the walls with seepage, they live with the Greek fella, I think they're from Denmark. They're a bunch of Huguenots and they're full of their old ways. Who the hell brought those dolphins in here? I smell eardrops. Get off my galleon with your pointed oars. I can hear the voices again. I will not sell oil to partridges any more.
WHERE IS MY MAP OF WHITECHAPEL?..........

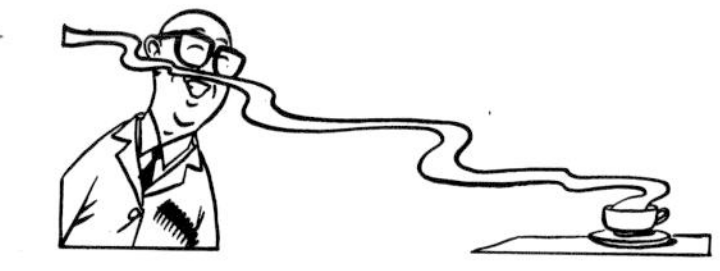

Les loves the smell of freshly ground coffee.

HOW TO SPOT A FOP

I first met the Fop in 1983, shortly after I was forcibly ejected from a rehabilitation unit in Slough. This eviction is in the hands of my lawyers. Unfortunately, the government has refused me legal aid on the grounds of a cathedral being on my chest.

TEN WAYS TO SPOT A FOP:

1. A terrible overpowering smell of lavender as they mince past you on the street.
2. In conversation they maintain a complete and sickening belief that their point of view is correct.
3. Personal documents such as a passport can be revealing and should be checked for exaggerations in height and about their ability to fight.
4. Fancy ways . . .
5. An adoration of Coconut Mallow, Gypsy Puffs, Philadelphia Cheese and Parma Violets above all other foods.
6. A tendency to gently suck baby foods through silk scarves.
7. Net curtaining around shoe collection.
8. Those stupid glasses with flowers on.
9. They prefer low-wattage light bulbs in boudoir.
10. Silk scarves often found beneath rabbit hutch.

REEVES AND MORTIMER PRODUCTIONS

Poor Quality Pantos for Peasants

SCENE 1

It was Xmas Eve in a disused rabbit hutch in Billingham, and Little Baby Jesus lay asleep in a tub tended by Mutha Goose (played here by Mary Quant). He was listening to his favourite Holy Jazz Fusion tape, when all of a sudden a mysterious figure wearing a shroud appeared and nicked off with the cassette, causing great distress as it was Jesus' favourite.

The scene was witnessed by Romantic Raymonde who was Jesus' agent.

JESUS: You soft get. You allowed that mysterious shrouded figure to nick off with my favourite Jazz Fusion tape, you must be punished.

And, behold, Jesus squirted some tart lemon into Romantic Raymonde's eye, causing him great distress.

JESUS: If you don't retrieve the Holy Jazz Fusion tape, I'm afraid I'm going to be forced to sack you, so get a bliddy move on.

Romantic Raymonde didn't know what to do. But wait, what's that on the floor, a clue? It's a piece of paper dropped by the shrouded sprinter.

ROMANTIC RAYMONDE (reading): Report for cleaning duties at Windowlene Factory, Nottingham, Winter 1566, signed Robin and Roy Hood. How the dickens do I go forward in time fifteen centuries? Perhaps if I ring this magic handbell...

And, indeed, he did ring the bell and was transported to the year 1566.

SCENE 2

Fifteen centuries on, Romantic Raymonde turns up in a disused wood near Nottingham, where he bumps into top international bass guitar wizard, Stanley Clarke, who was in the wood gathering berries and weeds with his manager, Wyatt Earp.

ROMANTIC RAYMONDE: Tarry a while, bass supremo, withy the way to the Nottingham Windowlene Factory, I charge thee?

Wyatt began to do an elaborate tap dance whilst Stanley joined in with some intricate Jazz Fusion music. Earp was tapping out the directions in Morse code, first the general direction, then the area, then post code and height above sea level, etc. Romantic Raymonde understood this coded message as he was Swiss, but there was a price to pay: Wyatt squirted tart lemon into Raymonde's eye, temporarily blinding him.

Scene 3

Romantic Raymonde went into a lemon-induced coma and slept for exactly one month. He was woken by the delicious smell of "Old Bruno" wafting down from Little Lord Fauntleroy's pipe (played here by Tom Robinson).

Fauntleroy: Good day, sleeping and yet romantic stranger.
Raymonde: Hail, Lord Fauntleroy, pray dither no longer and speak. Where Windowlene factory?
Fauntleroy: I am shop steward at factory. There are problems there as Robin Hood the boss is using a Jazz Fusion tape to brainwash the workers into making sub-standard bottles.
Raymonde: Bingo! I need tape for Jesus, give keys to office, I go, you come quick.

And off they scampered to the Windowlene factory.

Scene 4

Romantic Raymonde and Little Lord Fauntleroy arrived at the office of Robin Hood and began to rifle through his drawers, where they found the Holy Jazz Fusion tape. After a couple of hours, in burst Robin Hood (played here by Nat King Cole) and the factory production manager, Courtney Pine (played by John Sessions). Romantic Raymonde is put on trial! Little Lord Fauntleroy leaves, making a low moaning noise and a Pete Townshend-type windmill action with one arm whilst the other punches the air. Also his backside moves in a mysterious way, pumping and thrusting like a deranged beggar. Everyone leaves the stage.

The trial was over, sentence had been passed, and Romantic Raymonde had yet another squirt of tart lemon in his eye, and as we all know, three squirts of tart lemon sends a man back in time.

Scene 5

Back in Billingham, up popped Raymonde.

Raymonde: My liege, Jesus, Jesus, I have the Holy Jazz Fusion tape, my job remains secure Hurrah! Hurrah! and you my lord are happy again.
Jesus: Get with it, Raymonde, everybody's listening to Folk Rock in Billingham these days, not Jazz Fusion. You can take your tape and stick it up your fat arse. I've got a new agent now. Squirt him, Mingus.

The shrouded figure squirted Romantic Raymonde in the eye with more tart lemon and, as we all know, four squirts of tart lemon make a man a top indie record producer, thus guaranteeing Raymonde boardroom involvement with 4AD, Rough Trade and Mute, a managerial position with The Cocteau Twins, and continued sexual liaisons well into his eighties with Lisa Stansfield and Muriel Gray.

FOOD LACK INCIDENT
HOWAY, VIC, MAN -- YOU HAVEN'T FED US FOR A WEEK!
IT'S NOT MY FAULT! LES HAS FORGOTTEN WHERE HE PUT IT!
WAIT A MINUTE -- THERE'S A RIPE PIGEON NESTLING ABOUT 7 FURLONGS AWAY!
SMART!
NIGEL PARKINSON
CUMBAYA, ME LORDY, CUMBAYA!
92 SYCAMORE AVE
VISIT LISTERS MASSAGE PARLOUR DOCTORS, SOLICITORS, ETC. WELCOME Tel: KINGS X 9079
OH NO! IT'S THE FOP AND HIS COHORTS! I'M OFF!!
LA! LA! LA!
LES -- EFFECT PIGEON DISLODGEMENT WITH YOUR SPECIAL BUGLE!
HEY! HEY!
PROOOO
TOUGH LUCK! TRY YOUR STICK, MAN WITH THE STICK!
-- BUT THE STICK IS TOO LONG --
-- AND DISLODGES ALFRED HITCHCOCK, FILM DIRECTOR --
-- WHO IS FILLING HIS TALC HARNESS WITH POT-POURRI ON THE MOON --
HEY! HEY! HEY!
BINGO!
-- THIS GIVES ME A TOP IDEA!!

HEY! HEY! LEG, GIVE US ONE OF YOUR HEARTS!
DELVE
RUMMAGE
GOT IT!
THIS SHOULD DO THE TRICK!
HEY! HEY!
WHAT THE DICKENS--? THAT WAS A DECOY PIGEON!!
OH NO!
YES, REEVES-- THAT WAS MY DECOY INSTALLATION--
--USED TO ENTICE PROFESSIONALS TO MY MEDICAL POSTER!
HEY! HEY! HEY! I AM THE MAYOR OF CASTERBRIDGE AND ORDER YOU TO BELAY!
HUH?
HEY!
THIS MAN HAS BEEN PESTERING PROFESSIONALS IN THIS PARISH FOR TOO LONG!
GOH!
I CAN'T THANK YOU ENOUGH!
--YOU AND YOUR MEN ARE INVITED TO DINE WITH ME!
HEY! HEY!! HEY!!!
HEY, HO, HANDBAG PARAMEDIC TOFFEE-SQUAD!! TUCK IN, BOYS---I'M OVER 3 CENTURIES OLD AND I'M A MEMBER OF THE NECKLACE FAMILY! HO HUM!
OH NO-- HE'S RETARDED!
SEED
SEED
SEED

LES'S LUNCH CLUB

Turin Shroud
6 in gong used to alert trespassers
PROPERTY OF CHRIST
5 BEEF PROCTORS
You know them corn circles? They were made by me and my sweet heart simply rolling in the hay.
2 PLUMES Previously Les' eyelashes
Salt
Arc of Covenant
Makeshift tent mincing Hacksaw bulb.
After Dinner 'Fun' Funnel
Tree widths are based on my torso plus one old half-crown
YOU LYING GET
YOU LYING GET
I am THE GREAT RIFT.
I am MONT BLANC.

GRAHAM LISTER

I, like most doctors, dentists and architects, dress in a traditionally smart manner.

1

My hair is comb-plumed by a Greek man who lives in the flat above me.
The unique 'carefree curl' is achieved by the application of minute amounts of his phlegm.

2

My spectacles are only required for 'distance work'.
If I am at the lido or selflessly assisting staff at the local primary school, I wear my tinted glasses to avoid 'glare'. I am a fanatical reader and subscribe to *People's Realm* and two other specialist magazines.

My views are essentially conservative and I reflect this in my dress.

8

General Health. I've been on invalidity benefit for the last seven years. I did my back in pulling a nasal hair. I have to get my certificate stamped every second week by a doctor, he has to stamp it. The last seven doctors I've used have been completely incompetent and haven't been able to diagnose a terrible pain I suffer in my back. I subscribe to the BMA and I get the journal of the BMX, full of pictures of the operations.
I've got five complaints at the moment against the local health authority for negligent diagnosis. I've got terrible skin-flaking from anxiety over answering letters about bedding I've supposedly purchased. I suffer from one of the most awful cases of pediculosis known, that's lice, lice in general.

3

In my pockets I carry pins and the addresses of local primary schools. I keep all my money in there – I've usually got £30, a variety of membership cards and certificates, and rubber stamps. Because of my somewhat old-fashioned appearance, I'm often refused entry to places that need me. I have my lecture notes, as well. You never know when I might be asked to deliver a lecture on 'How to Take on the Town Hall' or 'Easy Ways to Pay Your Television Licence'. Leaflets from the Post Office, my Under-26 student railcard and my OAP bus pass, a pack of Handy-Andies. An eraser. Chalk. My mouth organ. A spare glass eye. A needle and thread. Breath freshener. A Body Shop voucher for my leg oil. A penknife.

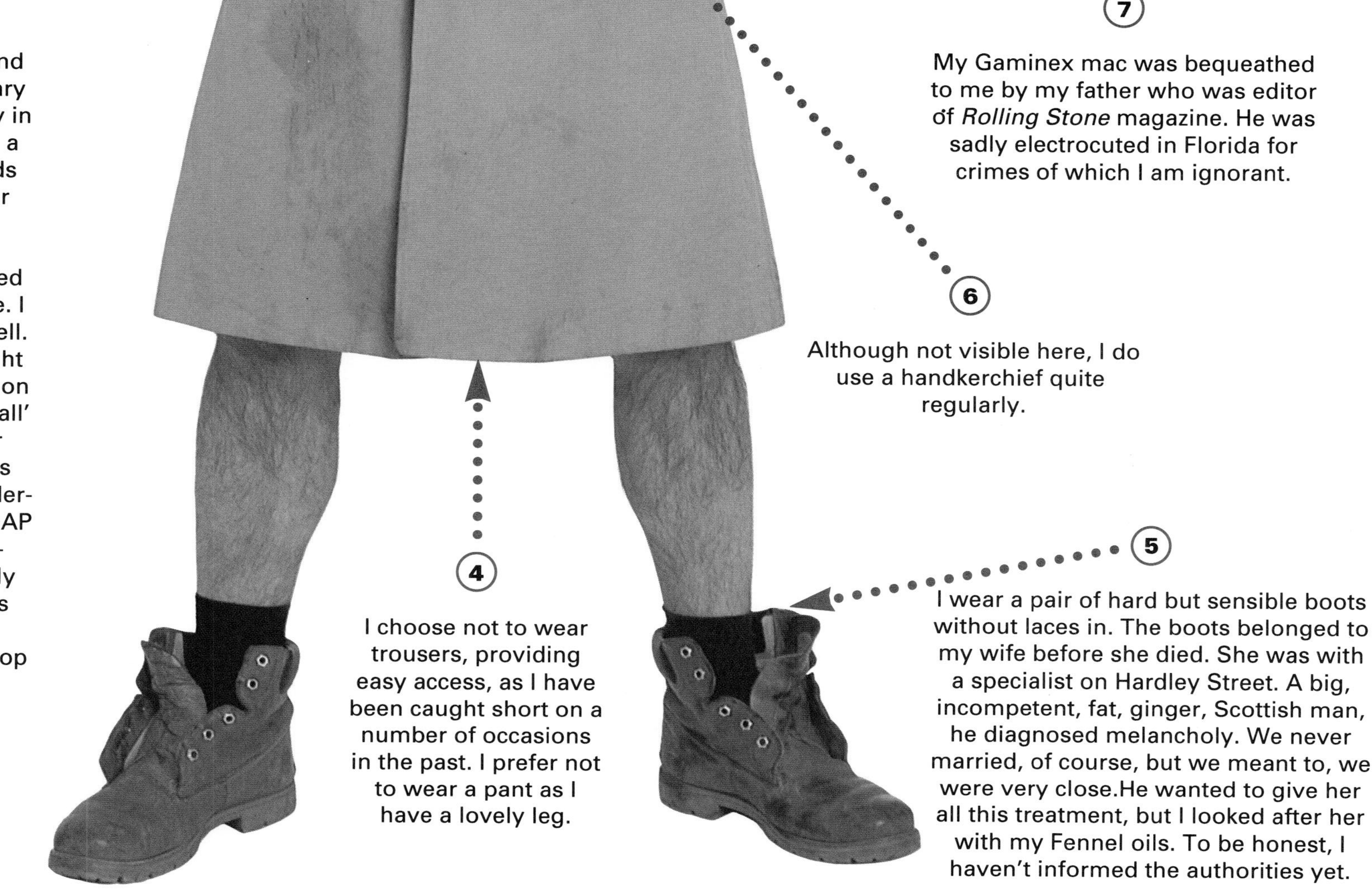

4

I choose not to wear trousers, providing easy access, as I have been caught short on a number of occasions in the past. I prefer not to wear a pant as I have a lovely leg.

7

My Gaminex mac was bequeathed to me by my father who was editor of *Rolling Stone* magazine. He was sadly electrocuted in Florida for crimes of which I am ignorant.

6

Although not visible here, I do use a handkerchief quite regularly.

5

I wear a pair of hard but sensible boots without laces in. The boots belonged to my wife before she died. She was with a specialist on Hardley Street. A big, incompetent, fat, ginger, Scottish man, he diagnosed melancholy. We never married, of course, but we meant to, we were very close.He wanted to give her all this treatment, but I looked after her with my Fennel oils. To be honest, I haven't informed the authorities yet.

A bright, clean, wholesome view. A sane voice in a sea of drivel.

DENNIS SIGNS ASWAD

Hello, my name is Mr Dennis and this is my confectioner stroke tobacconist shop. It is on the edge of town by a roundabout and near a park. I purchased the shop from my father who was apparently a rather violent man.

I don't stock CurlyWurlies as they are far too elaborate. Nor do I stock bread or cakes, far too fancy, but the sign does entice pensioners into the shop, as does the seductive smell of urea seeping through my wife's surgical bandaging (which I really must remember to change one day).

The door to my shop is slightly buckled due to urea absorption. I remember I was quite riled this day in particular.

However, I always have time for children, who I love.

The day I signed Aswad, I had accompanied my wife to the toilet. When some louts began baiting me about the strong smell of urea lingering in the street. This made me quite riled.

I decided to pop them one. The most aggressive of the bunch tried to land one on me. I quickly applied a thigh wrench to the throat, being careful to avoid chafing.

All smiles now. The louts revealed themselves to be top reggae pop group, Aswad, and heartily agreed to my offer of an exclusive promotional contract.

They didn't have a chance as I used an ancient technique to disable the wirey ones. No fuss or dramatics, a relatively straightforward popping executed clinically and with full chafe avoidance.A simple celebration. Nothing too elaborate.

We were soon off to their first gig. Yes, Aswad are now my boys and here they are live at Wembley Stadium. Another successful Dennis Promotion following on from Bad Brains, Lush, Ice T, Lawnmower Death and NWA.

PRRRAT!!
LOOK AT THAT!

SOME MEAT, SIR?
MAY I SUGGEST BRISKET?
IT'S O.K.

IT'S WARMED TENDER,
STICK IT IN YOUR BLENDER

Lovely Meat

Fresh meat

R.I.P. HUNGER
TWANG!
IT'S A TENDON

WOW!
BOILED HEN...
USEFUL.

BOING!
GOODNESS
GRACIOUS
MEAT!

BANG!
WHAT'S THAT ON MY PLATE?
HOT MEAT!

ZAP!
SLICED SWINE...
HANDY!

Hey! Hey! Hey! It's Meat!

REEVES
WHERE
PROFIT
COMES
FIRST
MORTIMER

THIS IS TOMORROW'S WORLD!

Exciting things are happening in the world today, things to do with aeroplanes and space, electricity and motor vehicles, radars and batteries. Who would have thought ten years ago that men would land on the moon and wireless transmissions would be received by even the very poorest and dirtiest of squatters?

'But what of the future, by jingo!' I hear you cry. Men have already travelled at speeds in excess of 160 mph and are currently making plans to conquer the mighty ocean. Where can we go from here? Let's take a good look...

By the year 2000 there will be no more houses, as we will live on floating platforms known as 'dwelling rafts'. These will drift about on the oceans because all the land will be used for giant airports.

In the future we will have no use for CLOTHES as we will no longer need our eyes due to telepathy and will all be blind, therefore we will not have to cover up our privates. Before this, however, we will be forced to adhere to strict nudity laws imposed by Bernard Cribbins, who will be the Minister for Temperance and Decency. We will have new clothes made for us by armies of blind musk-rats living in gigantic concrete grapes filled with boiling fat. They will weave elaborate brassières and underpants out of lemon rind and wire wool. During winter we will hibernate in test tubes made out of a milky substance extracted from dolphins' beaks.

SHOES will be made out of the skins of billions upon billions of wasps by teams of specially trained Hells Angels, who will live in pewter shacks on the moon. They will fire the shoes to earth once a week by cannons powered by explosive kidney beans.

By the turn of the century, the most stylish man and woman will be Rod Hull and Emu and Gloria Estefan, who will wear suits of armour in the shape of taps.

HAIRCUTS will become a thing of the past, and people young and old will develop protective crusts upon their heads.

'Where would we be without MEDICINE?' I hear you chant. Ah yes, where would we be, the Dark Ages? In the future, David Bowie and Lou Diamond Phillips will be the first two males to conceive children... by peacocks.

CRIMINALS will have a field day, as by the year 2000 the police will be preoccupied chasing a giant lemon that gazes through people's letter-boxes.

By the year 2000, DOMESTIC ANIMALS such as dogs and cats will have become extinct due to the new Councillor of the Exchequer, Colin Welland's, bizarre views on health. After he has introduced his controversial new bill, they will all be destroyed in elaborate golden clamps that he will personally administer.

Genetic research will provide us with a new type of household pet that will be part-turtle, part-Tupperware dish, part-cauliflower, part-children's Wendy house, part-bridge, part-leather thong, part-Welsh valley and part-gas. It will breathe only once a day and catch its droppings in a net woven from the hair of a virgin.

At midnight the thing will leave a trail of saliva and wood chippings around the dwelling to ward off evil spirits and at dawn it will wink at you to put you in a good mood for the day ahead.

FARM ANIMALS will be replaced with giant balloons filled with fat.

DINOSAURS will reappear in 2005 due to gales of up to 300 mph blowing them out of their underwater lair which has kept them hidden for over 700 years.

A trip to the CINEMA will be an intimate affair, as they will hold only three people at a time who will sit behind each other on stools made out of toast watching a blank, triangular screen made of cast iron and suspended from girders by a type of edible wool. After about two hours they will see a vague image of a musk-rat on some skis and

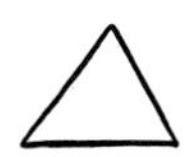

LES FACT ····➤ Les thinks triangles are dreary.

they will begin to chatter and emit a strong odour of fennel.

After we have visited the cinema, we may go for a MEAL. This will probably be at one of the new restaurants woven from magnetic shoelaces by specially trained tigers who, incidentally, may also go on to build huge new parliamentary buildings out of shredded wheat and nettles, glued together by human waste.

Our favourite meal will more than likely be a dish of lemon-flavoured Formica served by a kind of robot duck with a net on its head for catching the cherries that we will use as currency.

COOKERY in the home will remain both a necessity and a top pastime, although due to strict nourishment laws imposed by actor/writer John Junkin, who will be the King of all England by 1995, we will eat only scallops and privet leaves. These will be boiled into a thick soup in enormous oak vats hewn into the shape of The Brady Bunch and stirred with bass guitars by talking lamp-posts from the Planet X.

RICE will be individually coloured by trained horses, painted by hand in enormous communal silk wigwams.

Tomorrow's VEGETABLES will look like Henry Moore sculptures and be made out of meat for convenience purposes.

We will have our MILK delivered by blind half-man half-lizard-type things who live in cellars and pump it to the surface.

DISCOTHEQUES will be held in a well six miles deep and thick with fog. We will climb up and down the well, listening to a low hum that will have taken the place of music.

After a night at the discothèque, we may wish to BUCK. This, however, will have become impossible by the twenty-first century as our privates will have dropped off due to gale-force winds reaching speeds of up to 300 mph, so instead we will turn to another popular pastime, that of stuffing shanks of mutton up the exhaust pipes of hovercrafts.

Treasured above all else will be SPIT. It will be kept in exotic pewter jars and displayed at enormous eisteddfods held in Herefordshire.

And, finally, looking a little further ahead:

BIRMINGHAM will become AUSTRALIA and all CARS will explode at midnight. OWLS will rule the earth and everyone will live in giant RUCKSACKS carved out of LEMONS grown on the sun and driven to earth by two-headed FLAMINGOS dressed in floral nightgowns.

And as we head home to bed on our tiny little rubber tractors, we may reflect on days of yore and quietly smile to ourselves as we remember. And yet the simple pastime of friendship shall remain paramount in a world that doesn't care. THIS IS TOMORROW'S WORLD!

THE STOTTS

Donald and Davy Stott Interviewed by Cockerel, Inventor of the Hovercraft

LES FACT ··················► Les is part-Turkish, part-oil, part-tusk, part-egg, part-jewel.

But it is his Bryan Ferry dance which makes him unique.

Tell Me About Your Background

DONALD: We are twins. I am a bit older, however.

DAVY: Yes, Donald is three months older than myself. I was born in 1812 overture, so I am forty.

DONALD: I was born in 1941, so I am definitely forty. We don't like to mention this, though, as it can put the girls off. We were born in Shildon, the North-east, Durham.

DAVY: Our dad was a gypsy.

DONALD: No he wasn't, Davy man! He worked on a railway, and in the evenings he would go out with a dead tarty woman. He would return covered in pigeon feathers.

DAVY: We take after our mam. She was an Indian princess.

DONALD: She was lying, man Davy!

DAVY: No she was not. It is you who is lying, Donald. She had jewellery which sparkled.

DONALD: Stop starting, Davy! You're lying again, man!

DAVY: We were brought up in the first Barratt home.

DONALD: Davy, we were not!

DAVY: And I used to park my Triumph sports car outside it.

Were You Happy as Children?

DAVY: I was used as a child in adverts. I had to advertise apples. Apples out of the trees, that type. It was for the Apple Marketing Board, that is situated at Durham Tech.

DONALD: You did not do any adverts. You did not start speaking until your teens. He did not do adverts, he had to go to the hospital every week.

DAVY: I had Teflon on my arms.

DONALD: He had the water on the brain thing.

DAVY: It was Hydrofoil. They had to drain it off.

DONALD: I was quite brilliant at school, but I was thrown out. First Davy was thrown out for lying, and then because I am a good fighter, I went and popped the teacher.

Did You Have Problems Earning a Living?

DAVY: I worked for the Duke of Marlborough, servicing and flying his helicopter. It was bright orange with diagrams on it.

DONALD: Stop starting, man Davy! He's lying again. We went straight out to work at Lowcock's Bottling Plant factory at the end of the street. We used to go round on the delivery van.

DAVY: I stopped and worked in a shoe shop. I was the brightest spark in the shoe industry in England. I invented a shoe – I got the idea from a road going into the distance.

DONALD: That's always been one of Davy's best things, his sense of style.

DAVY: I had to leave, though. I didn't know you had to take money from people.

Did You Earn a Decent Wage While You Were There?

DAVY: Yes, I earned two thousand pounds a day.

DONALD: He's starting again!

DAVY: It was two silver thousand-pound coins. That is what I was told by Roland Judd who owned the shoe shop.

DONALD: When he sacked him I went and filled in Juddy, using a cup. He owned the Bottling Plant factory too, so I was made redundant. By this time our mam had lost her kidneys.

DAVY: And her eyes.

DONALD: And her ears.

DAVY: I made two new eyes out of the eyelets in shoes and two marbles. They sparkled.

What Caused You to Move Down to London?

DONALD: Our dad moved in with a woman who stank to high heaven.

DAVY: She stank of milk and light-beige biscuits.

DONALD: We went to the Job Centre and saw a sign saying, 'Come on Telly and be a Star. Signed, Vic Reeves'.

DAVY: Judith Grant from our town went down too. She had to keep her hood up because she is bald. She was after his marzipan. That's why she went bald. She handled his marzipan.

DONALD: Davy man, don't tell the man that! Marzipan is private!

DAVY: We got the Rapide down to London and stayed with our Uncle Pete in a Sally Army place. There was lots to eat.

How Did You Spend Your Time in London?

DONALD: We went to see Mr Reeves, but we were a week early, so he made us wait. He kept us busy, like, cleaning his chimney. His chimney is 300 feet long. He lives in a factory.

DAVY: I was invited to the Queen's house within an hour of arriving in London. She asked if I would like to be King, but I said, 'I simply haven't the time, Queen.'

DONALD: We had been living in a house and paying rent to a man called Graham Lister, but it turned out that it was really owned by five big ginger Scots. They became Genesis.

DAVY: I nicked one of their skirts, however, and that was when I started making jokes. I said 'Donald, where's me trousers?' and he said, 'I'm wearing them!'

DONALD: He is a funny man, Davy Stott. Tell the man some of your jokes, Davy.

DAVY: Waiter, the soup is too thick! No, sir, it's an omelette! My arms are so long, they're fifteen foot long! Waiter, there's a biro in my soup! No, sir, it's a sausage!

What Are Your Talents, Donald?

DONALD: I am a good fighter and I used to assist the police. I would crawl in the bushes looking for clues. To date they have not taken up any of my clues.

DAVY: Donald also has evidence that pirates existed. In the shape of a coin.

DONALD: Don't mention that, man Davy! One day I will be very rich through pirates.

DAVY: Donald also wrote *Tarka the Otter*. He made it up out of his mind.

Do You Have Relationships With Women?

DAVY: Donald has a girlfriend, but we know what she's after.

DONALD: You say she is mercenary, but I am stylish and you just can't take it.

DAVY: She's fishing for your marzipan. And she has no hair.

DONALD: Davy goes out with a sixty-year-old woman.

DAVY: You shut up! She has no lower jaw, I'll admit to that. She can't speak very well. At all, in fact. She is often mistaken for a pelican.

DONALD: She is called Old Sally. We like strippers, especially Big Margaret. She has a big bum and a big belly hanging over. She has tassels like eggcups.

What Does the Future Hold for the Stotts?

DAVY: I have been invited by Lord Belmont to ride on his horse shooting otters,so I will go.

DONALD: Stop starting again, man Davy!

DAVY: And Lord Longford has invited me to his house to bludgeon otters, and the King of England has asked me to go to Scotland to kill all the deer.

DONALD: Stop it, Davy man! Mr Reeves says that we are his favourites. He invites us up to his house to play in his toilet. Mr Reeves looks after us.

DAVY: No, Donald. It's not true. I've seen him rifling through your haversack.

DONALD: Oh Davy, not another marzipan mercenary!

DAVY: I stopped him, Donald. I shot him with a tranquillizer gun I got off Lord Longford and then I moved it to a lock-up I borrowed off Minder.

DONALD: Thank you, Davy. I love you, Davy.

DAVY: I love you too, Donald.

VIC'S FRIENDS FROM THE ANIMAL KINGDOM
HELLO EVERYONE, DIGITAL CLOCKS £5·99P.
MORRISSEY THE CONSUMER MONKEY
B*S F*****H
CAPA! CAPA!
NIBBLES THE COMEDY DUCK
ALAN DAVIDSON THE FOUL-MOUTHED FOX
Oh No, what am I doing in this publication my wife's going to KILL ME!
GLEN MITCHELL THE GORGEOUS SANDY-COLOURED LABRADOR
WOT! NO RABBIT

BIRTHDAY PRESENT WORKSHOP

So, there's a birthday in your family, but you're too poor or idle, or perhaps even a council worker with plenty of time on your hands, or you're trying to make amends for a terrible family error committed during the harvest-festival period with a nephew. Well, here are a few present ideas that I've come up with:

1. FOR GRANDAD

Handy Storage Units,
Four marge tubs labelled 1-4 (in blue, representing a ringmaster at the Big Top) to store:

a) tools
b) slippers and pipe
c) dressing-gown and ointments
d) top hat and cane and a foam-backed numerically-indexed personally-coded wallchart numbered 1–4, so he knows which is which.

2. FOR DADDY

a) Two sycamore leaves Sellotaped together make an ideal glove. You might want to make two of these for a pair, but that depends on what sort of a budget you are working to.
b) A length of toilet paper makes an ideal scarf. If it's a cravat Daddy prefers, that can also be constructed with the same materials. Either way, try not to use a soiled length as I once did.

3. FOR MUMMY

Why not treat her to a flour-and-lager face pack, and for exfoliation just mix in clock parts, used teeth, segs or Blakeys, winnits, fuse wire (toss the fuses in as well... and the fuse box), zips, curtain hooks and any old rubbish out of the garden. Stick it all in a bucket, mix it up, and after she's tarted herself up with the paste, she can use the bucket as a nice hat.

4. FOR LITTLE JOHNNY

Get all the family to chip in, and buy a pre-packed sandwich for his birthday tea. Cheese or egg is usually the cheapest, but shop around. Keep the transparent harness, fill it up with used grass, put a peg on it, glue it on to Johnny's back, and tell him he's one of those Kung Fu turtles. When the fad's worn off, rip it off, sell the grass and it makes a nice school cap or turtle lunchbox.

CAN-U-WINK?

Yes
It's Good

SEE, it
works
good

NO!

TRY OUR NEW

WINKING STICK

VIC 'N' BOB TALK POP MUSIC

Come with us through a few of the choicer moments in popular music.

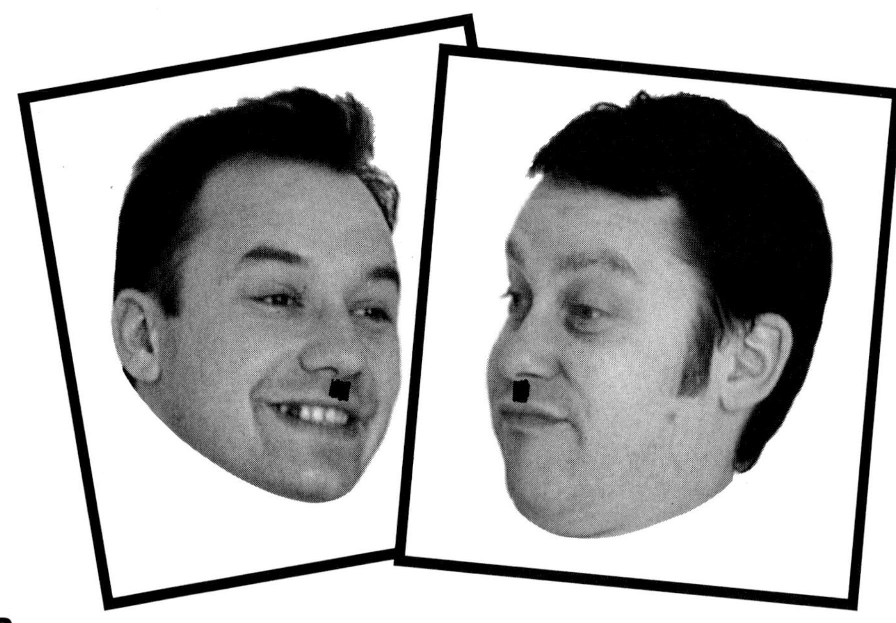

THE CURE
Disintegration

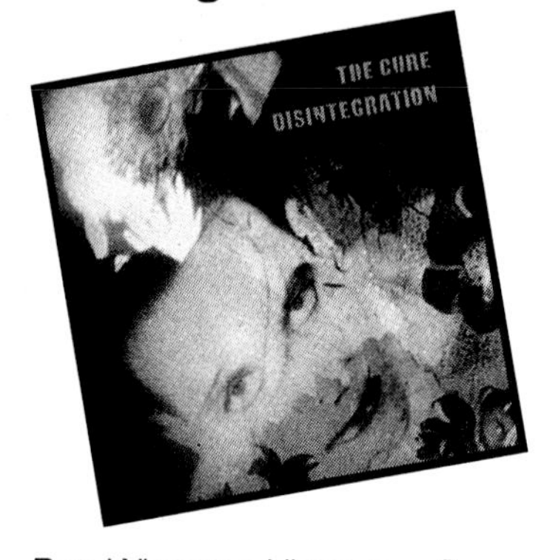

Bob: Whenever I listen to a Cure album, it's like walking into a cathedral.
Vic: It's a shame he's got a voice because the music's quite smart. This is the sort of music you get when a new hot and top king is crowned.
Bob: His new tent's been built and he's got his flag saying, 'I'm in now, come and buy something off us.' People can't resist applying make-up when they hear this music. He's as old as us now, this fella. I don't think they've ever been given the credit they deserve for championing the middle-class squatty movement. They could have died away without the likes of these, you know.
Vic: I saw him wandering alone on Regent Street with all his make-up on, he looked such a sad sight. I think he's got some sort of machinery that he puts his head into.
Bob: If you had the choice of going out with a lass who liked The Cure or a lass who liked Bowie, who'd you go out with?
Vic: Cure.
Bob: Me, too. I'd shoe a horse to this sort of song. I'd hum it in me mind whilst I was being told off by my boss for having all this stolen food in my pocket. It's all whisper whisper with Robert, innit? The lyrics aren't very literal. I like bands who give orders, 'It's good fun to get up late? And go to the bookies/ Then eat some cream.' You never get any instructions. I think when he sees us he sees our skeletons and that's his secret. That's why he's in such a terrible mood all the time. When he was young he used to burn Majestic Wafers in front of the fire and then lick the chocolate off and spit it at his gran. That's what gave him the idea for The Cure because that was the cure. She used to twitch when the runny hot chocolate hit her. He'll lose his hair, Robert.
Vic: He'll lose his face if he's not careful to keep out of winds. What's his name, Robert Fox? Robert Wood? Robert . . . what's his name?
Bob: What are prats called?
Vic: Smith! Robert Smith.
Bob: His hair is never quite right. He's teased and he's teased, but he's never got it quite right. He's gone for a rich plume, but always a hair out.

PUBLIC IMAGE LTD
The Greatest Hits, So Far

VIC: Hello, hello. It's nice to hear someone saying 'hello' at the beginning of their records, but I don't like his big suits. When he went over to Los Angeles he had a decent head of hair, but now he's gone for a Rod Stewart plumage. He's been there two weeks and he's got down Fanny's hairdressers and over-teased. Sad. It's a particular lip he's got.
BOB: I don't think any bands are really angry. It's a personal thing. You can be furious with your neighbour 'cause his tree's dropping leaves in your garden, but I don't think you can be angry with the world.
VIC: I liked it when he pretended to be Led Zeppelin, that spot! But after that he dipped, maybe he'd eaten some food that was off. He's got the best face in pop music.
BOB: No he hasn't, he's got a common face.
VIC: There's nothing wrong with common faces. Do you have to have a posh face to be in pop?
BOB: Susan Peefer out of The Bangles has a better face.
VIC: No, he's got a better head, look at the sleeve.
BOB: He looks like a West Brom fan. Alex Harvey and Tony Hadley had character in their faces.
VIC: He looks like a mad twelfth-century monk. If he'd been born five hundred years ago, he'd've been dead.
BOB: I'd play 'What's it All About' to startle an owl that was bothering me.
VIC: I'd listen to it whilst slicing pears for a dinner party.

KRAFTWERK
Autobahn

BOB: This is the diary of a journey on a motorway. Did you go and see them at Musworth Town Hall when their names were up in neon?
VIC: No, these are foreigners with technology and they always use it that little bit better.
BOB: They've seen the future.
VIC: My favourite's Ralf.
BOB: The balding one. Do you remember the Milk Race song they did? Brilliant.
VIC: There was a video of them all riding round on bikes like robots.
BOB: They live a brilliant life, don't they? In a little sealed box.
VIC: They're German, but the bloke in the car is Dutch, he's on a search for sex. Dutch farmer on an endless search for sex and embezzlement. It's all done on corrugated iron, this music. During a yoghurt frenzy. Their next album should be something for the English, 'A Glimpse of Something Chequered' or ' A Taste of Tweed'.

THE FALL
I'm into CB

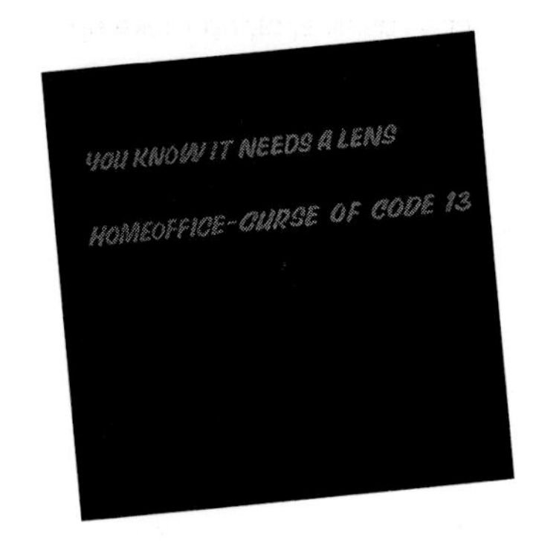

VIC: He's the jacket king and he hasn't lost it. He always wears black slacks.
BOB: I am ignorant of The Fall. I find him difficult to listen to. I always like The Fall when I'm at a club, but at home I listen to The Best Of . . . and couldn't get away with it. I find it irritating.
VIC: I sit and examine the words. In all the years I've listened to them, I always find something I haven't heard before.
BOB: They're serving a different need to the need I have from music.
VIC: You prefer a more fluent banal lyric and a melody. I like the bell in this one, that's Mark Smith hitting the keyboard player on the head with a triangle. 'Jaw Bone' and 'The Air Rifle' are top songs. This is soul music as far as I'm concerned. I think he's hilarious.
BOB: I think he's probably got very good eyesight, and he doesn't use it.

DE LA SOUL
3 Feet High and Rising

VIC: I like this album.
BOB: So do I. It's badly produced though, the sound quality's crap.
VIC: They were the first ones to come up with a decent tune, they changed the face of Rap.
BOB: Gang Star have followed these up.
VIC: When I'm in the bath, I'd get these to sit in front of us and sing Simon and Garfunkel songs.
BOB: I'd like to go on a country walk with them, somewhere there's a pub. I think they'd have their own drink, though, in a flask. Malt drink. I bet they eat a load of jam straight off a plate. I think they'd have three good chefs, brilliant team. None of them would slack. They'd know instinctively when one had done enough washing-up and they'd change and he'd do pastry.
VIC: Whilst the other gave a lecture on freshwater fish in Britain. They'd make good church wardens as well.
BOB: If they ran a lido, it'd be a good-fun lido.
VIC: No sharp rocks.

THAT'S JUSTICE!

VIC: 1776. Abemtifishiglen in the Scottish Highlands, a gorgeous wee ginger virgin girl weeps neath a terrific outcrop known locally as The Devil's Terrific Outcrop mourning the abduction of her only child ('Ginger') by a headless pig from a nearby pub. In a search for justice and equity she has come to the outcrop in the hope of an audience with the Laird.

For three weeks and three nights she waits and weeps spilling tears of despair that fall unnoticed on to the barren land neath the outcrop, known locally as The Devil's Terrific Outcrop. Drained and desperate she makes her way wearily to a nearby pub, slowly she opens the gnarled and twisted timbers that maketh the door of the pub known locally as The Devil's Gnarled and Twisted Timber Door and enters.

'My Laird, will ye not find my wee bairn for me?' she cries for it is he. But mercy is not upon his menu this night for he dines with a headless pig upon wee Jamie McCrylic, the child of the virgin of the outcrop known locally as The Devil's Terrific Outcrop.

What days were these when justice was a whip and a chain, a rat-filled well and a curse uttered from the swollen lips of a bloated pox-ridden landlord hell bent on sexual athleticism and filling his gout-filled thighs with heroin and gin?

And let us now re-create those days as we enter the rubicon, handbag, marrowfat tick-tock world of Judge Lionel Nutmeg for

THAT'S JUSTICE!!!

LES FACT ····► Les once chased a crab up an alley!

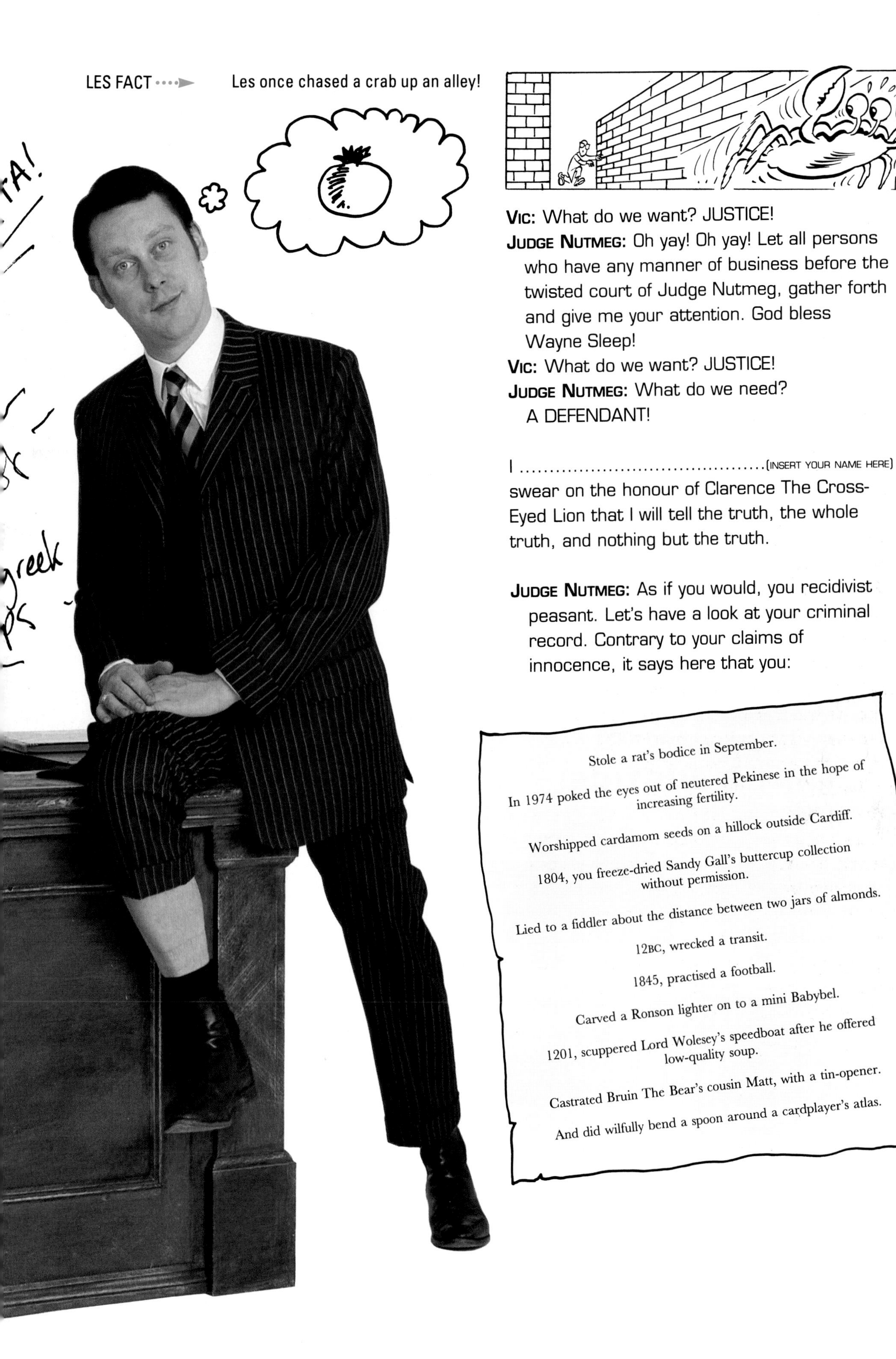

Vic: What do we want? JUSTICE!

Judge Nutmeg: Oh yay! Oh yay! Let all persons who have any manner of business before the twisted court of Judge Nutmeg, gather forth and give me your attention. God bless Wayne Sleep!

Vic: What do we want? JUSTICE!

Judge Nutmeg: What do we need? A DEFENDANT!

I ....(INSERT YOUR NAME HERE) swear on the honour of Clarence The Cross-Eyed Lion that I will tell the truth, the whole truth, and nothing but the truth.

Judge Nutmeg: As if you would, you recidivist peasant. Let's have a look at your criminal record. Contrary to your claims of innocence, it says here that you:

Stole a rat's bodice in September.

In 1974 poked the eyes out of neutered Pekinese in the hope of increasing fertility.

Worshipped cardamom seeds on a hillock outside Cardiff.

1804, you freeze-dried Sandy Gall's buttercup collection without permission.

Lied to a fiddler about the distance between two jars of almonds.

12BC, wrecked a transit.

1845, practised a football.

Carved a Ronson lighter on to a mini Babybel.

1201, scuppered Lord Wolesey's speedboat after he offered low-quality soup.

Castrated Bruin The Bear's cousin Matt, with a tin-opener.

And did wilfully bend a spoon around a cardplayer's atlas.

Judge Nutmeg: Why do they do it? Why do they do it?

Vic: What do we want? JUSTICE!

Judge Nutmeg: What do we need?

Vic: THE WHEEL OF JUSTICE! Bring on the wheel!

Vic: What do we do with the wheel of justice? COMB ITS HAIR! Let's have a look at the punishments on my gorgeous penal wheel.

Judge Nutmeg: Spin the wheel, you deformed and dangerous crofter!

Vic and Judge Nutmeg: SPIN, SPIN, SPIN THE WHEEL OF JUSTICE.
SEE HOW FAST THE BASTARD TURNS.

THAT'S JUSTICE!

JUDGE NUTMEG CV

Born 1431, Raffles Hotel, Bangkok.

After serving as a senior strategic military adviser with various armies and dictators including Visigoths, Picts, Gengis Khan, Cromwell, the Khmer Rouge, Papa Doc and with that South American fella that didn't like HM, he fled to England and commenced a career at the bar.

His rise was meteoric and greeted infamy with open arms as he developed the Nutmeg Penal Code. Extract:

> **Kill all first-born with fish slice.**
>
> **Arbitrary destruction of all woodland.**
>
> **All deers to be clamped and pounded with golf and hockey balls.**
>
> **All menus to commence with crabsticks.**
>
> **The poor to be forced to wear traffic cones on their heads and be employed to detonate landmines at Goodwood Racecourse.**

The people of England couldn't get enough of it, and he was quickly promoted to the office of Lord Chief Justice On High Oh Yes, M'lud. It was here that he passed some of his most innovative and spectacular sentences on some of the country's most vicious criminals, including Oscar Wilde, Nelson Mandela, Alexander Solzhenitsyn, Wat Tyler and Emily Pankhurst.

Judge Nutmeg now lives at 1715 Crofton Avenue, Bath, Glos. with a young Turkish boy and a little Scottish terrier called Mengelies. He has no children.

He holidays in Eastern Europe, Libya and Mesopotamia and has a vast collection of antiques.

LES FACT ··········➤

Les once beat the living daylights out of a jellyfish with a pair of ballet shoes!

SIMPLE STORIES

An Agatha Christie Mystery

1. 'Look, someone is hiding in that thick reed-bed. Do you suppose they are a murderer?'
2. 'Never mind them. Look, there is a burglar hiding in that Scots pine tree.'
3. 'Oh, Christ.'

The Rally

1. 'Good afternoon, my friend. I wonder if you can help me. I'm looking for the vintage traction engine rally.'
2. 'Certainly, sir, carry on up the lane and you are at it.'
3. 'I beg your pardon, old chum, but I am never "at it".'

Murder at the Black Mansion

1. 'Somebody in this room is a murderer. No one must leave until I give the order.'
2. 'But, officer, I need to go to the shops for some Opal Fruits.'
3. 'Oh, very well, sir.'
4. 'Thank you, superintendent, thank you.'
5. 'Don't mention it, sir.'
6. 'Oh, all right.'

Top Cop Drug Story 1

1. 'Hi! I'm Mike Dukas of the NYPD. We'd like all you people to leave the building as there's a dangerous hooker in the neighbourhood.'
2. 'Excuse me, officer, but I gotta keep my bagel shop open in order to git by; ya see, I got a wife 'n' kids.'
3. 'Hey! I recognize you, you're Don Wright, the criminal.'
4. 'Aw shoot! I knew you'd get me sooner or later.'

Top Cop Drug Story 2

1. 'Hey, Dumas, we got another one in a used-car lot on 49th and 7th. It looks like a No 1 with a sprig of parsley on top.'
2. 'OK, Jack, grab a coffee and we'll nail this greaseball with a pine-cone and then take 5.'
3. 'You got it, buddy, this time it's personal.'
4. 'That's right, Jack, this time I ain't gonna take no crap from Lomax without wearing rubber gloves.'

Top Cop Drug Story 3

1. 'You sure are one classy broad to be hangin' around with a scumball like Tony Peretti.'
2. 'I could close this joint down tomorrow, Lomax, now what's the name of Fat Joey's sponge?'
3. 'Hey, Lieberman, you got some nerve feedin' me this crap when your wife's playin' midnight skittles with a cheeseball like Johnny Duke.'
4. 'I'm goin' in alone, Murphy, cover my ass with pellets if it all goes off.'

ACTION IMAGE EXCHANGE

Action Image Exchange (AIE) are Nick Adams (23) and Nick Price (22). They met accidentally at an accommodation agency in Leicester, where both were looking for a flat prior to commencing degrees in Mineral Engineering at the local polytechnic.

Nick (23) is the bossy one, whereas Nick (22) is quiet and thoughtful. After several 'blind alleys' and 'wild-goose chases', they found a one-bedroomed flat suitable for sharing. The landlord was a fat Greek man who was always showing them obscene photographs of himself.

Nick and Nick soon found that their grant cheques didn't 'stretch' very far, and realized that it was the government that was 'to blame'. They held a meeting above a pub. Only their landlord

turned up. He wanted his rent. More sparsely attended meetings followed, and with them more controversy. Inevitably, arrests occurred.

1.4.88:

Nick (23) held in police custody for forty-eight hours simply for the crime of printing a recipe for dope cake in his local squatters' newsletter.

7.8.88:

Nick (25) held 'illegally' aboard a police tug-boat simply for the crime of cuddling a yew tree with some of his bisexual Druid friends.

1.1.89:

Nick (22) spent one month in prison simply for the crime of sharing out some dope cake to some Druid animal rights protesters picketing a Wimpy poster in El Cubador.

3.4.89:

County Court Judgement £415.27 fine for non-payment of rent by Nick and Nick.

8.5.89:

Nick (21) one year community service for indecent exposure.

'Enough is enough,' said the boys, and they went 'underground', emerging only occasionally to do their thought-provoking performance pieces on the Vic Reeves show. They have produced three leaflets explaining their path to political growth, entitled as follows:

1. *Why We Like the African Tube* (1989)
2. *Photographing Your Own Genitalia* (1990) *
3. *Fighting the System From Within – Why We Choose to Work at Texas Homecare* (1991)

LADIES AND GENTLEMEN, ACTION IMAGE EXCHANGE:

Action Image Exchange now demonstrate their performance piece, 'The Facelessness of Bureaucracy' aka 'Shapes'.

The accompanying soundtrack alternates between Swing music and the sound of wind.

* written jointly with Yamous Poppodinkusous

LES FACT

Les stows his Weetabix in a bright red kennel!

Flipper Represents :-
1. A foreigner's view of life
2. A Badger winking into a handbag
3. A honey bear infuriated by the late arrival of her holiday tickets.
4. A flipper
WORLD WOR II... IT WAS JUST CRAZY MIX UP!

MAN WITH THE STICK

MY MATE TERRY

Vic: So, Man With the Stick, come in and put your stick down. I believe you're now going to tell us a bit about yourself and your good friend Terry.

Man With the Stick: Yes, I am indeed, Vic. Some say that he treats me bad, but if you've got someone that you like, that can make you laugh all the time, then they're worth having. Terry's hilarious and he's popular with the lasses and that.

He's very good with voices. Once he pretended to be the boss at work and said to me, 'You're sacked.' So I left, and didn't get me proper job back. Then he often pretends to be a lass. He goes, 'Man With the Stick, show us your willy.' And I think it's a lass, so I get it out and it's usually the boss.

He always finds work for me though. He makes me Tipp-Ex the stains off the walls, cut all the serrated edges off stamps – he reckons he gives the little bits to charity, scratch the boss's car, then splits on us.Probably does, he's a nice fella.

Terry keeps getting promoted because I do the bulk of his work, you see. He's got nearly right to the top, and I know that whilst he's there he wouldn't see me bad. I don't really want promotion. It's like Terry says, you know – who needs it?

He's got a brilliant side-parting, mind. He creeps up on the lasses, gets them pregnant, then blames it on me. I pay him three lots of maintenance and he puts it on the horses. Then there's me house. When I was on holiday, Terry's brother moved in there, beat me up quite bad. I applied for an injunction, but I used the solicitor that Terry put us on to and he beat us up quite badly an' all.

Me money from me wages is supposed to pay the mortgage, but Terry arranged that for me with an accountant, and so all the money was going to Terry's stud farm. So the house got repossessed, put up for sale, and Terry moved in. Got it cheap because it had all been wrecked by his brother with his parties, and his circus, and his cannons.

Now he does concerts from there, I can come in at the end and clean up for him. Sometimes I sleep in a tent round the back, and during his parties they come with their syringes and inject drugs into me for a laugh and play at digging holes into me stomach. The reason I live in the area is because I like to be able to visit Terry; I pass by, but if he's in with the lasses, they throw stuff at us.

LES FACT 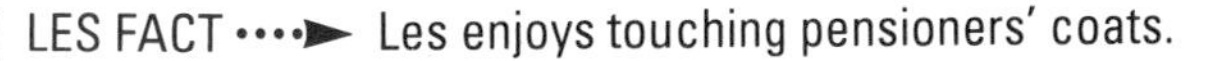 Les enjoys touching pensioners' coats.

Of course, I've got me kids, but they're in a home now. I do get to see them, though on me last five access visits, I've been out working for Terry.

Terry gets richer and richer. I've never understood it because Terry sends me bills every week for £148 per child, but they're in care and as I understand it the local authority pays. It's a proper invoice so I pay it – I'm a respecter of invoices. I know it's always going to be clerical work for me, but it's much more fun working with Terry. He lets me colour in graphs, and I do the leafletting for his charity work in Bolivia. I deliver lots of packages for him. I pay for them, but I do keep the receipts.

I was doing these food-poisoning tests with Terry and I nearly lost me arm. He injected a bull into it. I have a skin-graft at the top of me thigh where Terry booted us once for a laugh. What they made me do was sit on the photocopying-machine and photocopy it until it got really hot and melted.

It was Terry that got me on to the drink. I didn't invite happiness into my life, Terry just came along. Life's been more than I could hope for. I never knew me parents, but Terry's parents and mine knew each other. My parents used to live outside his parents' house. I'd be on the rubbish tip without Terry, and I'd have less responsibility at work, but I'd have a bit more money.

MAN WITH THE STICK SONG

Man With the Stick:
This year's works holiday
was two weeks away in Greece.
It was all arranged by Terry
who gets flights cheap.
I did not find out about it
till the day before they left.
No details on the notice-board –
I was completely in the dark.

Vic:
When he got on to the plane
his bag was full of heroin
Terry had planted there the previous day.
He told him it was sherbet
and he ate the flippin' lot.
His head swelled up, he farted
and destroyed the flamin' jet.

Man With the Stick:
When I got back home
my job had been taken by Terry's brother,
and the bank manager had repossessed me house.
Apparently Terry had paid for the holiday direct
from my current account.
No details had been sent to me –
I was completely in the dark.

From the secret notebooks of Doctors Slater and Hunter

THE MAGNIFICENT AROMATHERAPY TREE

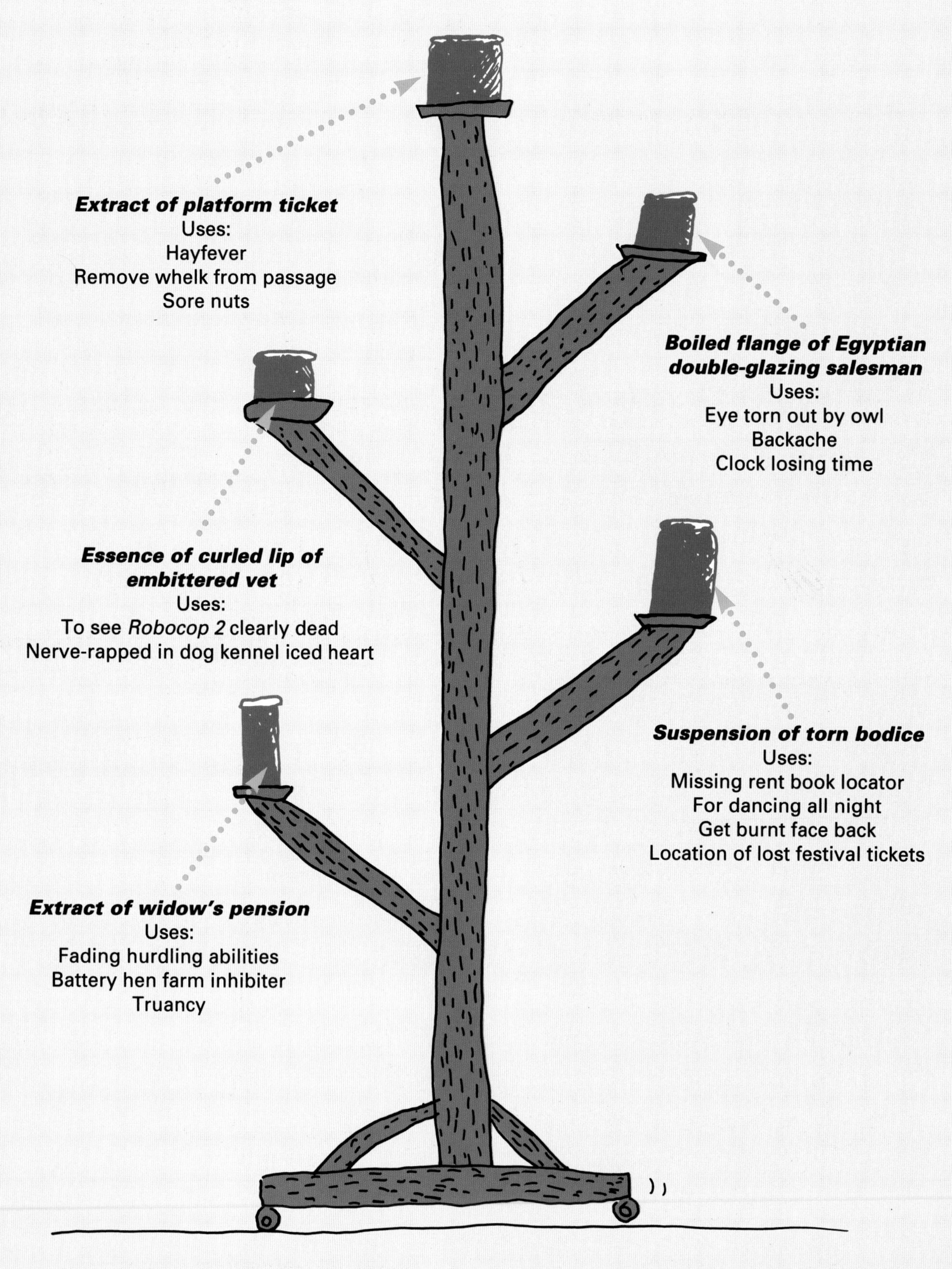

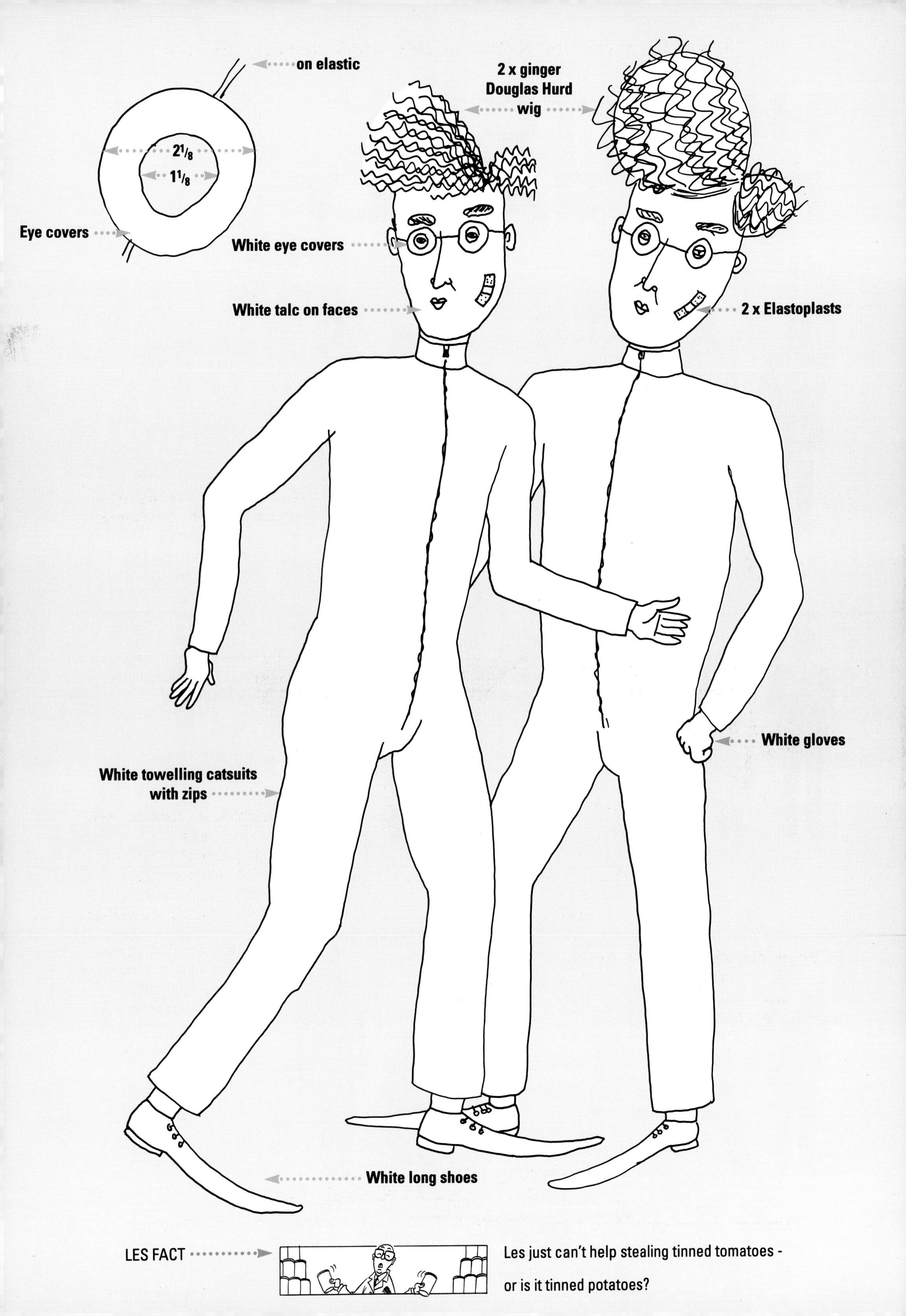

on elastic
2 x ginger
Douglas Hurd
wig
$2^1/_8$
$1^1/_8$
Eye covers
White eye covers
White talc on faces
2 x Elastoplasts
White gloves
White towelling catsuits
with zips
White long shoes
LES FACT
Les just can't help stealing tinned tomatoes -
or is it tinned potatoes?

HOW TO FALL SAFELY

RIGHT

1. Upright and attentive posture including intense and obsessive concentration.

2. Sudden realization of oncoming fall. Mouth widens to alert passers-by. Arms well tucked in to avoid turbulence at 15 (Nemesis point).

3. 30. Appropriate foot access computed, selected and held. Legs held together to avoid sweetbread entrapment.

WRONG

1. Bob's mind is wandering, his thoughts are on other matters.

2. This leaves him vulnerable and leads to a slight weakening in the right cartilage.

3. Excess weight on right side provides no buttress to incoming fall. Chafing unavoidable as right knee connects with hardened kitchen work surface.

LES FACT ··········►

Les is well-respected in a subterranean kingdom near the earth's core.

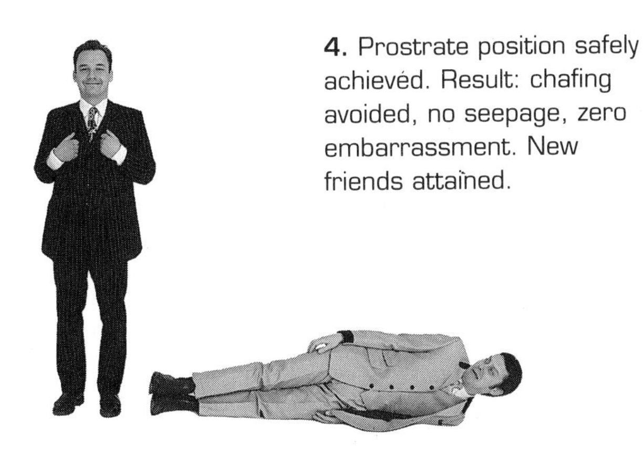

4. Prostrate position safely achieved. Result: chafing avoided, no seepage, zero embarrassment. New friends attained.

4. Thigh connection leading to rear hair lodgement including excess lathering and seepage from back knee sweat gland.

5. He thinks it's all over. Bounceback achieved for realignment.

5. Cries for pity and sympathy will go unheard due to blatantly incorrect falling technique. Result: excess chafing, friends lost, nerves frayed.

BOB: Hey, Vic, sorry to interrupt the falls and that, but I'm really down in the dumps.
VIC: Why, little one, whatever can have caused this singular malaise in one so spritely and gay?
BOB: I forgot to fluff up my pillow when I made my bed.
VIC: I know how you feel. I didn't wash up my nutcrackers after I'd used them this morning.
BOB: Oh no, you must feel suicidal!
VIC: I do, man, I do.
VIC: And you know what, Bob?
BOB: What?
VIC: I DON'T CARE! Ha! Ha! Ha!
BOB: I know! NEITHER DO I! Ha! Ha! Ha!
BOTH: Ha! Ha! Ha! Ha! Ha! Let's go! Ho! Ho! Hee! Ha!

VIC'S POP PAGES

POP STARS' HAIRSTYLES

BANANARAMA
The three singing daughters of Kate Bush first made their name in the mid-fifties as 'Emerson, Lake and Palmer', changing their name in 1987 and becoming an immediate success with their hit single 'Hotel California'. Having recently changed their name again to 'Earth, Wind and Fire' after the three seasons, they hope to swim the Channel and have sexual intercourse with Mike Yarwood.

1
Phil Oakey: The cascading side flange, featuring a jawline twistgrip rollback, covering a vent.

THE POLICE
Three schoolchums from Ireland, Sting, Stuart Adamson and Clive Chappel, had nothing to do in their school hols. They all had guitars, so one day they decided to go into a neighbour's garage and bash about. They were consequently arrested and spent five years in remand centres. When they were released, they formed the Police and had a hit.

THE HUMAN LEAGUE
When Steeleye Span broke up in 1965, flautist Philip Oakey and singer 'Mercury' formed 'The Human League' with Billy Idol. Their first hit was 'Vienna' with Olivia Newton John. Their trademark was Oakey's lopsided flange which flapped during performances. They recently dug a massive trench around Britain, and hope to fill it in with tightly packed wool.

☆☆☆☆☆☆☆☆☆☆☆☆☆☆☆☆☆☆☆☆☆☆☆☆☆☆☆☆☆☆☆

2
Barry White: Double-oiled and ploughed ridge-back pyramid featuring disc beard. The disc beard is obtained by shaving round a tin of tomatoes or, if unavailable, a tin of butter beans, a digestive biscuit or a beermat.

TOP POP FACTS!

One of Teeside troubadour Chris Rea's kitchen tiles has lifted up a bit. Chris is going to try doing it himself before getting anyone in.

✸

It's a big con! The Proclaimers are singing Scot Brian McTaggart and a highly polished full-length mirror!

✸

Due to alopecia, Fish of Marillion is selling his home-perm kit this week in *Loot*.

✸

Apparently Paul McCartney, D. Bowie and Sting all live in quite big houses.

✸

Sheena Easton has a face like a little chipmunk!

3
Aha's Morten Harket wearing the unique 'Cherries in the Arch' coif, also known as 'The Ladies' Favourite'.

4
Crazy punk Billy Idol sports his favourite style 'The Gooseberry Bush'.

Ode to Gilbert (O'Sullivan)

Gilbert O' my Sullivan,
I love the songs you sing.
Ooh, baby, I'm a writer not a fighter
Oooh wacka doo wacka day
I'm alone again naturally
where the peaceful waters flow.
We will get down Claire
and discuss matrimony.
No matter how I try
my father is
alone again naturally.
Oh Gilbert and Richard O'Sullivan
please get down once again.

MR DENNIS AND GRAHAM LISTER

DENNIS: Well, I appear to be in charge now, though I don't know why they've invited me into this publication. I don't, in fact, approve of letters being put together in the form of words, as all letters are, is elaborate shapes used to distract people from their workaday lives and draw them into some form of hypnosis. I've been serving the community for some time; when has an author ever served us? Not likely! The only lettering I will acknowledge is on packaging, done in a vivid primary colour. Or the announcements that the circus is coming to town. I look out for that particular word linkage. I enjoy boxing magazines, but I just look at the pictures and adopt the relevant stances. I get my friend Lister to write letters of complaint if need be.

[Enter Graham Lister]
LISTER: Yo! Respect, Dennis!
DENNIS: Respect's due, Mr Lister!
LISTER: Of course it bloody is, of course it bloody is. Anyway, Dennis, how is the little shop and wife?
DENNIS: The shop's doing very well, thank you.
LISTER: There's a terrible putrid smell coming from the back, Dennis. How is your wife? I used to look forward to hearing her bubbling.
DENNIS: It was a gurgling.
LISTER: OK, I'll drop it.
DENNIS: Er, are you coming to my Midsummer Impro-Free Form Jazz Festival at Romney Marshes? People have to swim out to the arena.
LISTER: Thousands of lives were lost last time you organized an event like that, weren't they?
DENNIS: Let's not go into that. It didn't get publicized, of course.
LISTER: That's because you own half the media, don't you, Dennis?
DENNIS: I also provide the poles for The Dream Warriors now, you know. And I write all the songs for Roachford. I've just been laying down a bass line for him at the manor.
LISTER: I've just signed up Burn-Out, myself.
DENNIS: Oh, I'll put something in my publications. I've just taken over *Esquire*, along with *DEF II.*
LISTER: Do you still run BettaSpecs?
DENNIS: I do, and I shall shortly be selling flotation

LES FACT ····➤
Les knows a superb little Italian restaurant.

tanks, some new chemicals, and cider.
Lister: Very nice. I hope it all goes well for you. Do you like Gary Clail, Dennis?
Dennis: I've got no time for him. He spouts views which I find quite unnecessary.
Lister: Yes, he is a bit of a ranter. I've signed him, unfortunately. I can't get out of the deal.
Dennis: I'll be able to get you out of that one, because the ON-U Sound system is in fact owned by myself.
Lister: Oh, lovely. By the way, Dennis, I'd like to take your wife to see The Pixies. I've got front row seats at the Corn Exchange.
Dennis: The wife can't come.
Lister: She came with me to see Todd Rundgren. And Talk Talk. We had to leave because of the Dettol vapours. I haven't seen her for some time, Dennis.
Dennis: Er, I'd like you to write a letter for me.
Lister: Have you never thought about attempting to treat your wife with one of your flotation tanks?
Dennis: Drop it.
Lister: Of course you haven't. She'd sink, wouldn't she? All those holes from the trepanning you did.
Dennis: That's quite enough about that matter. Could you write a letter of complaint to the Milk Marketing Board for not attending my Ride concert?
Lister: I don't have the materials. Your wife could jot it down, Dennis.
Dennis: Don't rile me, Lister.
Lister: You're a stupid man, aren't you, Dennis?! You can't read or write! It's bloody preposterous!
Dennis: Don't start me, Lister!
Lister: You're a bloody fool! I've got something on you now!
Dennis: You'll keep that side of me quiet! I can pop you, Lister! Remember what happened last time! No one riles me!
Lister: Come on, Dennis, back off! Respect!
Dennis: POP! You don't start me! POP! I'm started now! POP! I'm vexed!
Lister: Aaarm! Aaarm! Aaarm!
Dennis: Had enough, have you, had enough?
Lister: Help! I require assistance! Damn you, Dennis!
Dennis: Who's next? Do you want some? Eh?

PETER GABRIEL MEETS ERIC MORECAMBE

Hello, I'm Peter Gabriel, and I'd like to take time out now to read you a poem on a subject close to us all, namely world ecology. It goes something like this:

Plip. Plop. Hissss.

Silent but deadly, the acid rain falls
upon a peaceful Norwegian wood.
Plip. A barn owl is struck by a blob.
Plap. A fox gets it on the neck.
Plop. A bat is splashed by the awful sprinkler
of death.

[Morecombe enters at about this point]
But I am safely tucked up
in my space-aged metallic live-hut
full of turnips and chocolate for me and my girl.

[Bob turns and sees Morecambe]
Bob: Wha!
Bob: Oh no!
Vic: Way hey!
Vic: Arsenal!
Bob: Why do you do it?
Vic: Hey! Hey!
Bob: Right, forget it then.
Bob: Sometimes I think you deliberately try to make me look stupid!
Vic: But you are, Bob. You are a complete and utter idiot.
Bob: Look, everyone thought I was Peter Gabriel with one of his special public service announcements.
Bob: There was some children out there and I'd just about brainwashed them into thinking I was a caring man.
Vic: You mean to tell me that you thought that they thought that you actually thought...
Bob: Yes.
Bob: I know that, but you didn't have to tell them, did you?
Bob: Anyway, what's in that bag?
Vic: Oh, it's just a fruit cluster I brought to cheer you up. I thought you looked a bit peckish.
Vic: Here, open up wide and have a snack.
Vic: Hey! Hey!
Bob: Ooh!
Vic: Take it, man.
Bob: Mmm, thanks, that was yummy yummy. Anyway, Vic, are you still diverting those funds from Heart Research into your Otter Fur Bookmark business?
Vic: Shut it! You had to mention my endangered species/stationery outlet, didn't you? You wouldn't let it lie.
Bob: I would have let it lie!
Vic: But you didn't let it lie!
Vic: Fa fa fa fa fa fa fa fa fa fa fa
Vic: Rooaaaghh!
Vic: Scroot scroot scroot
Bob: Shut it, homeboy. I'm off and I'm taking the fruit cluster!

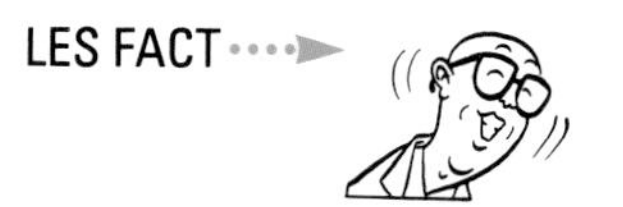

Les reckons that a fire extinguisher brings good luck.

What is on the end of the stick?

Ipswich?!